Notes of the Heart

Marian Griffin

DEDICATION

I dedicate my book, "Notes of the Heart" to my mother who loved to write and always encouraged me to share with words and creative processes. Starting when I was a very small child my mother wrote and read as she shared her love of the written word. She is no longer with me in this physical world, but I feel her huge heart which inspires me daily.

I also dedicate this to my spiritual teacher who instills her love of humanity to me as a way to teach that anything is possible and that everything comes from within the scope of the heart. It is in this place of longing that I write the words that I have often been taught with great sincerity and love. When I am centered in my heart I am able to see the good in everyone and in myself despite the challenges that I may encounter. In this way, my wonderful teacher has shown me that we learn through our tribulations especially when we are able to make the best of what comes to us. In this way, each challenge makes us more aware of the greatness that is this amazing Universe and elicits our trust in the Highest Self. We are blessed when we see the good that can happen regardless of the difficulties that may present themselves to us. We grow and we continue on this journey to the inward God in this way with great humble hearts.

I dedicate this book to those that I've worked with over the years as a teacher for every single person that I've worked with has had something to teach me and has been an influence on my life. Although, I've loved teaching and the children have shown me continuously wondrous things teaching as a profession has been hard work that can be physically and mentally exhausting. It is a way that I have given back to society and has been extremely fulfilling mostly because this kind of work brings the teacher to his or her own center. It is the kind of work that takes great heart because it comes from the heart. With that said, I am inspired by those who have shared their thoughts about children, teaching, fellow teachers and their lives in general. I have been fortunate to have amazing fellow teachers who have touched my life.

I dedicate this book to my family members who have shown me inspiration in the most sweet ways with laughter and with tears. I have felt blessed to have family in my life who have cared and reached out to me regardless of time, distance, disagreements, silliness, laughter and with awe-inspiring shared thoughts. I feel very lucky to have a family who cares for and about me as part of the group that we call "family." I learn through all of my family members who have shown me great patience, kindness and love throughout my entire life.

I dedicate this book to good friends who have come my way throughout my life. I have been blessed by people who have shown their hearts and their sweetness when I've been under the weather, sad, hurt as well as throughout the very best of times. I treasure the laughter that I've been able to share with good friends as well as the times that have given me great pause for contemplations which have taught me ponderous life lessons. I've been honored with wonderful friendships throughout my life and some of these have continued since my childhood. I am grateful to have friends who feel to me as much a part of my "family" as are those people that were born into my "family."

I dedicate this book to the Earth that I am graced to walk on, the stars up above that illuminate and that I pray to, the

water that I drink and bathe in and the air that I am
fortunate enough to breath in.

I dedicate this book to God with all my humble and
thankful heart.

Introduction

The spirit dances inside the child. It sparkles with a radiance that is truthful, pure and totally free. The child is immersed in the light within that guides him to play in a land of bliss. This is inside all of us, but somehow we've forgotten it... Can we get it back?

When I was a child I had visions, dreams and a sense of intuition that I counted on. My spiritual journey in this lifetime probably began in childhood though like with many adults this was discounted as I "matured." Still, somehow, I yearned for what I once knew and with that started the process of learning about my inner guide when I decided to work with children. I held the role of "teacher," but truly these little ones taught me what I needed to know about myself and about life.

It is my sincere estimation that all children have a knowingness and as a young adult I began the journey to seek what it was that I also held onto as my "Truth" in childhood.

Delving into the journey of the internal and divine self exploration I became a teacher and then saw in the eyes of the children that I could make a difference. I knew that there was something in the child that was also in me and wanted to touch on this more profoundly. I wanted to know who the child was within everyone. It was then that I saw this spirit clearly as a recognition of the divine in all people and creatures. However, I had to learn to honor the highest within myself before I could fully give with the heart and this was how I began the adventure of delving into self knowledge. As I did this I found that there was an ongoing reflection of love that was deep within myself and further as this exploration continued I saw that this is the most true possibility within all people.

Through my work as a teacher I have been blessed by open hearted children who were companions of my soul. With these children an overwhelming need within me probed to go deeper and to connect on a spiritual level though this was just the beginning. It was the start that was yet to unfold to how I would probe inward to seek the spiritual connection of every person and animal that I was to meet. When this awareness happened my senses expanded and gave a new basis of learning and giving. I started to know that there was a progression that would unfold in a mystical though completely natural way. I began then to yearn for what was beyond what I had known on the physical plane, and yet, this divinity was there within my physical world as well. It was a magical dichotomy which molded my gift to be like a child whose spirit within was totally intuitive. Further, this newness propelled a spiritual life that sought the heart for connection in a way that didn't always involve speaking or even physical sight. Along with this yearning for connection knowledge was manifested of a deep place that resonated as the soul which connects all of us as One.

As I explored this process it revealed itself as one that is transcendent and is derived intrinsically. I began to know of the potential for greatness that was and is within me as well as within everyone else. I knew too that this expanded beyond the physical realm to what is the invisible, the "Heavens," angels, spirits, auras and the minds. Yet, today as my pilgrimage into the highest Self of all beings still continues I am finding that with an open mind and an open heart the world can be healed through the wisdom and purity of the child because of the child's openness to spirit. On a deeper level I hold that the adult also has this ability though it is cascaded in a myriad of fears. It is my hope for adults to give way to loosen fears' grip and allow the light of the greatness within to permeate again as this will benefit the child as well as the world because it is the adult that molds the child's perceptions. It is the adult that transmits these fears to the child and therefore ultimately holds the child back from knowing his and her own greatness within.

The mission, therefore, that I have undertaken is to know the teacher in everyone beyond the scope of the fear that presently permeates our society and holds us back from our intuition as well as from freely being able to express love for one another. This is a first step to an acknowledgment that the world is the classroom and that the classroom abides within those with the most open hearts.

Perhaps most importantly, I have learned to enjoy the process of experiencing what I have needed to grasp beyond what has been my challenges even within the most difficult times. In this way, I grew through internal inquiry and experimentation.

My goal is to share my wisdom with suggestions that may make living in this world more fun, easy and an avenue to tune into the highest Self. It is with honor that I share my love for the hearts with the most purity within as an offering into the union of humanity's greatness.

Coming Back To The Self

On the hottest day of the summer she jumped into the pond where she shook off her wings as if to fly though instead dove inward deep into the cool, crisp sparkling water. This was her haven.

She was a child who thought of herself as a fairy capable of anything. She could manifest her greatest desires when she simply concentrated on them. She believed that anything was possible and that she could read the minds of those who came near her. She felt their feelings as an empathetic girl and any boundaries that were set for her could easily be cast aside if she deemed this necessary. She knew that she could fly in absolute freedom to travel to far away places and to meet other children as well as her guides. Life was a dream that was hers to create for she was fearless and capable of any and everything.

On that hot day on her fifth late July she swam in the clear waters kicking with abandonment and moving gracefully. She threw the water around her laughing gleefully. Nothing could stop or get in her way of creating her play. She was a magical fairy in the making.

Ten years later she dyed her naturally blonde hair black to match the wings of the raven and she wore thick dark makeup that concealed her fair skin. Her clothes were completely cast in ebony and she pierced her nose, ears and belly button herself. This she held told the world to look out for her and that nothing could get in her way. She was a fierce force who believed in her own abilities to make her life her own through the potent power within.

She marched her way through the halls of her high school with stares from those who held useless fears from the students to the teachers. She knew that the knowledge within her was the truth and that this was her guide. She wasn't afraid to reveal what she needed at any moment as she laughed heartily when she recognized that she intimidated the so called adults with her audacity to live by her intuition as her guide.

She was a gypsy at heart who could predict people's futures with one glance though she knew that the only truth that she had to hold onto was her own. She was truly gifted.

Her parents, however, were afraid for her. The didn't see the beauty in the abundance of the creativity that she held onto with the freedom of pretense. They didn't see the value of her natural trust in her own intuition. They didn't think that she was "gifted" at all and they continued to tell her this in a myriad of ways.

"You will lose your friends." They told her this as if to imply that if she didn't attempt to fit into a mold that society had created, she'd be alone. "You scare people!" They warned her that people did not understand her "readings" and that they didn't appreciate being told that she "felt" things.

At first these warnings didn't mean much to her. She wasn't one to give up on herself easily, and yet, a very deep part of her wanted to fit in. She didn't want to be an "outcast." She loved people and she wanted to be loved in return.

She began to dress like how she observed that other people did and she stopped dying her hair. She looked like any other fifteen year old girl in the high school year book, and yet, she knew that she still had abilities to "know." She tried her best not to let on. She no longer freely told people what she picked up about them and she kept what she knew intuitively to herself. Still, she didn't see any harm in honoring her gifts as long as she kept this private. She meditated and she kept a dream journal because she knew that this part of herself was the most true part of her.

However, her mother told her that she was "Silly girl" when she caught her meditating. She told her that she should be out with other girls her age doing "normal" things. She felt shunned and she was shamed.

Another ten years later she graduated from college and entered into the work force. It wasn't easy because even though now she was well educated there were not many jobs for those just out of college. She set out to prove herself. She wore suits and professional hair styles. She worked hard and put in long hours. She did what she was told to do and she worked her way up the company ladder to create a reputation as a strong and honest employee. She began to make money and to buy things. She had a house and met a man who told her that he loved her. He was a few years older than she with a lifestyle that many admired. He was considered a success in life and certainly a "good catch" for any girl.

She grabbed onto what she could and she made due with a life that she had worked for though she was rarely happy. She didn't know why she felt as discontent as she did because by anyone's standards she had it all. She had the beautiful home, happy marriage, expensive sports car, ski trips, clothes, jewelry and much admiration, but she was never satisfied. There was something intangible that was always missing and this led to a feeling of internal sadness most of the time.

She didn't understand her feelings and often didn't even question them. Then, one day as if by chance she came across one of her old journals from when she was a teenager. She sat down and began to read her own words. She was taken aback by what she found in this little book written by someone whom could easily have been a stranger. It told of meditations and intuitive hits. It stated that she could manifest her dreams just by believing in them. It talked about seeing spirits around her that guided her and of a belief in an internal voice that never let her down.

Reading all of this she began to smirk as if this was ridiculous teenage ramblings, but despite her doubts she found herself coming back to this book often. There was something in these writings that she knew held a part of her that she longed for. She knew that this part of her was the aspect that held her deepest joy and she knew that she *had* to get it back.

From then on every morning she sat at dawn to meditate on her own greatest Self within her. She had visions and she began to hear her own voice of intuition again. She knew that this was the most accurate part of her life and that this was her divinity. She kept a record of what came from her mediations in a journal and she started to do yoga. She became in touch with that deep part of herself that she held so intensely as a teen and so joyously as that five year old fairy girl in the cool, crisp sparkling pond. She dove deeper and became One with her own spirit.

This is the story of how most of us sense our intuition with glee and abandonment as children. We take it for granted as it is simply who we are though as we "mature" and go through life it is often stamped out of us. We are taught not to take it seriously and to even fear it. We move through our lives with mixed priorities which lead to discontent because we have forgotten about the very essence of who we are.

It is the lucky person in this world who is able to come back to the spirit within and to honor that sense of intuition which is our greatest guide and gift to ourselves and to the world.

Once upon a time there was a little girl who preferred day dreams to the more "worldly" activities of those around her.

She was a pretty little girl with yellow hair as golden as a sunflower, big blue eyes, high cheek bones and a slightly turned up nose. People thought of her as a "good" little girl, but in reality this girl called Tinkerbell was spunky and full of mischief. She was the girl who not only wanted her own way but got it most of the time. Her emotions were intense whether happy, angry or sad which made her hard to handle and certainly challenging to deal with at times. Yet, she was also loving and sweet which endeared her to those whom loved her.

She also had skills. Tink could put pieces together from anything broken especially hearts. This talent often came in handy because people around Tink got themselves into messes because they hurt one another. They said things that wounded others and did things that injured hearts. Tink who could have just as easily flown in opposite directions took to these people. She wanted nothing more than to sprinkle her fairy dust on them so that they too could learn to fly and experience what it was like to be above the mundane. She wanted them to have her dreams of pixie love.

This was all good for Tinkerbell until one day when she met Peter. He was not like the usual boys that Tinkerbell had known. He appeared to be oblivious to her flirting which was extremely odd in itself. He was boyishly handsome and Tinkerbell was smitten from first glance. She dressed in her cutest green flock that showed off her girlish curves and flitted around him with her dimpled smile and golden hair in hopes that he would take notice of her.

Peter, however, had indeed noticed Tinkerbell's skills. He had seen how gracefully she could fly and how she was able to maneuver in and out of situations. He saw that she was also competent with people who otherwise were disagreeable. He realized that Tink was quickly adept at putting broken people back together and he admired this.

"Tinkerbell," Peter said one day, "I'd like to introduce you to someone." Tinkerbell agreed to fly with him and together they flew past the moon and into the clouds to another world where they met a young woman named, "Wendy."

Have you ever met someone who upon first meeting you decided that this was someone who you just couldn't appreciate? Wendy was this person for Tink, but Peter appeared mesmerized by her. This not only baffled the fairy called Tinkerbell but annoyed and even angered her.

Wendy was very unlike Tinkerbell. She couldn't fly to save her life and in reality was a very "grounded" kind of person. She walked with a steady pace and appeared to be completely direct in how she approached her life. Tinkerbell decided that Wendy had no sense of adventure, no spunk and no spirit to be able to fly with.

One day, Tinkerbell told Peter what she thought of Wendy. He laughed at first thinking that Tink was jealous though concluded that Tinkerbell didn't understand. He said, "Sometimes, I wish that she could be more like *you*." Tink smiled. "**But**," he continued, "I wish that you could also be more like *her*..." Tink looked sad. "Don't get me wrong, Tink... It's just that sometimes she's *so* grounded that she lacks something extraordinary that you possess and then you...well, you are just *so* flighty that I wish that you were more down to earth."

Tinkerbell saw in that moment that Peter loved both of them for different reasons. She knew that he saw the good and not so good about them both and that he loved them equally.

She knew that all the fairy dust in the world couldn't change Wendy and that she herself could never be completely "down to earth" either. She then realized that she *liked* the fact that she could fly and found that she *also* admired Wendy's steadiness.

Tink grew up to be a woman called Marian who is flighty at times and grounded at others. This woman, Marian can like Tinkerbell mend hearts and can break just as easily. Like Tinkerbell, Marian is strong willed and brave though also childlike and like Wendy, Marian is steady and decisive.

I am grateful for the Tinkerbell within because she has given me a sense of wonderment. I am grateful for the Wendy in me as well because she has made me strong and steady. I am the fairy who flies freely and I am also the woman who makes her life her own through steady and strong choices.

Once upon a time a fairy called Tinkerbell came to me and introduced me to a girl named Wendy. These two became my heros and today they live together in my heart as me.

Let Go And Choose Happy

When I was a child happiness came naturally and my mother nicknamed me, "Merry Annie." Happiness was a *way* of life.

I remember the joy of running down stairs to see my father when he got home from work, walking to school, touching the pussy-willows, and swinging on the swing so high that it scared my mother. Small things made life adventurous, but this changed as I "matured." These things vaporized becoming insignificant as bigger, more distinctive events needed to occur for "happy" to be elicited.

Happiness was no longer a way of *being* as an unconscious choice was made to be discontent as if this was stronger and more riveting. However, I find morose people **less** compelling. It doesn't take much effort to live one's life driven with fury, sadness and malcontent, but I want more than to exist. I want to *feel* life, to take it in and to be *with* life. In doing this, I know that we as adults can give 'happy' to children as well as to ourselves. I also know that this is important.

Once my life shifted in a huge way which scared me. First, I went into a survival mode. We *need* certain things in this world to get by, and this caused me sleepless nights of worry. I then went into a fighter mode which was required. It was productive because I was able to get what I needed and to make smart decisions, but, I slipped into depression. My emotions were that of failure at life, but *change* **is** *life*.

It took deep contemplation of the, "Everything happens for the best" resolution that I've adhered to in the past to elicit insight.

Fortunately, wisdom trickles down like rain when we are most dry giving us thirst quenching knowledge that is ultimately needed.

I had become absorbed in an egoistic reality of who I was as my role of "teacher." This function of who I thought that I was consumed me and took me away from the most basic aspect of my truth. Contemplation allowed me to see how the patterns of life's busyness had taken over as I strove to achieve aspects and to acquire others leaving *"I am that"* which is what I've learned through my spiritual teacher as the highest Self behind.

Yesterday, I spent an hour at the pool. I swam laps and floated. I felt free for the first time in a long time; unencumbered by life's expectations. I let go.

No one said that life was going to be easy. Everyone has challenges. This is karma. Karma is what we chose to learn before we came to this realm and there's no escaping it now. If we don't take in our lessons, the cycle will continue until we have at last processed what is needed to learn. Karma is a not bad thing. It is what we have *chosen* to become greater.

While at the pool I overheard a couple of men talking. One said, "It's about simplifying life." This resonated for me. Life is what we make it *emotionally* as well as physically.

As I strive for simplification I look to the things in my life that bring me joy. Still, there are times when even this is a struggle. Can you relate? Candles of beauty, light that glows in your heart, children's smiles and an elderly person's wisdom are all there for you, yet, a feeling of closure looms. You are immersed in this all consuming cloud, but why and where did your 'happy' go?

Life can feel like a huge tidal wave that you can't swim out from under regardless of your attempts to make "good."

I've experienced being immersed in feelings that life holds duality of "good and bad" causing agitation, however, life's challenges happen to take us further into our highest selves. It is in this place of darkness that we begin to shed our egos and to look to our hearts for the light that creates a way toward happy.

The other day I walked into my bedroom aghast by its condition because papers were scattered around, dirty clothes piled high and things needed sorting. It was a task that I didn't want to touch because it felt more than I could handle, and this space that wasn't made me feel suffocated. I dove in and it was cleared a half hour later and no big deal so why did I hesitate?

Have you ever felt tired on Sunday evening with Monday morning looming? Monday has not started, is hours away, yet, exhausts you. The chore of Monday or cleaning out the space isn't what drains us. We are spent due to the *energy* of the task ahead. This might be people, bills, worries, projects, etc., that deplete us long before they've been met or even started.

Sometimes I remind myself of that little girl who shrieks, "I'm scared" when she hears lightening boom. Despite my "sophistication" there is still that child who climbs under the covers to hide from loud noises outside of herself, but truly the scariest things are *inside* of us because the most frightening things are caused by our own minds.

My wonderful teacher wrote about allowing yourself to feel divine contentment with your courage. She said that this helps when your mind creates stories of fear, etc., because the reality is that this fear is a story in itself.

She also said that contentment comes when we know that God is both within us and that we are within God. She illustrated this by talking about a dream that she had where she was swimming and a huge tidal wave took her body spinning it all directions. I can relate to the feeling of being overwhelmed, but my teacher said that in her dream she didn't "struggle." She surrendered. She made a conscious choice to be content with the knowledge that she was protected. She had faith in this resolve and ultimately was not only fine but blissful.

It takes courage to make a *decision* to be content during times of challenge.

Yesterday, I watched a TV show where Jane Fonda was interviewed. Jane is in her seventies and said that she is happier than she's ever been. She said that she has developed "wisdom" with the knowledge that regardless of what comes up in life she will be fine. She smiled and said that this resolve was elicited from deep contemplation and added, "It's not enough to have experiences in life. You have to contemplate them."

We all have difficulties in life. This is part of life, but we don't learn from these times unless we see them as lessons and contemplate them. To do this we have to go inward and see what comes up for us that triggers our fears. My experience has been that when I am able to go into my heart I can witness my fear without its "Scary" emotionality and I am able to work with my fears. This helps me to confront the fear and remind myself of the times in the past when I experienced obstacles though got through them. This exercise derives my inner courage to know that I am protected and with this realization I am not only content but **grateful**.

Fortunately, there are tools that help us stay in the present moment and protect ourselves from energies that are not our own. Thankfully, these tools are right within us, free and easily accessible.

The first tool that I've found to be most beneficial is the breath that we hold as our life force which in Sanskrit is called, "Prana." Take long slow breaths in and out mindfully as you remind yourself of where you are physically and that you are safe. You can do this anywhere even at a meeting at work and no one will notice.

In private, sit in a chair with your feet on the ground and hands in your lap, take long breaths, look around the room, sense safety, close your eyes and go inward to your heart. Listen to the sound of your heart's beat and feel it's draw. Come to realize how large of a space that heart cavity is and imagine it growing more vast so that it holds all of you and everything that you hold dear. Stay in this place for as long as it takes for you to feel completely clear of any energy that pulls you from your own personal feeling of safety.

Imagine that there is light drawing from your feet and see it releasing into the earth. Let this ground you. See another light coming from the skies merging into your spinal column and cleansing back to the earth. Feel that your entire body shines with light infused within you and listen to your heart's beat. You are one with this drum and it is the pulse of the Universe where there is no duality. You are safe, nurtured and your highest Self.

Hold onto that light and let it beam into the world healing everyone and everything with your love.

Know that it takes courage to have faith in your own internal 'happy' and ride out obstacles with a degree of optimism. It's **not** easy.

Faith is often tested which is *purposeful* because this takes you to a deeper place to contemplate, do self inquiry and to *burn*. In the yoga that I practice we use the term "burn" often as something that is painful though beneficial. We also say that the spiritual teacher is "fiery." People can become confused when we say this and misinterpret it to be something negative which it's far from. To burn in this way is challenging and often a painful process, but it's also **amazing**. The spiritual teacher puts us through **fire** as she burns away our impurities to remove our Karma. We burn to become lighter *literally*.

Faith to follow one's own path requires a degree of surrender which isn't easy. You can't lay down to watch someone else do the work. No. It involves participation and trust. Remember that great philosopher, Mick Jagger? He said, "You can't always get what you want, but you get what you need." It takes faith to realize that *whatever* it is that you get is for the best.

Faith comes in many paths which doesn't always involve churches and this elicits a very deep sense of 'happy.'

I used to watch children as they attempted to work out conflicts. Their's was very simple. They'd scream at one another, kick, hit and even bite until one of the two gave in. One child would then cry while the other walked off in triumph never looking back at the crier. In a way, we adults are not far removed from this scenario.

Consider most conflicts that you've been involved in. There is usually an aggressor and a victim or at least the parties could be perceived in this way. Usually our squabbles are a bit more sophisticated than a fight over a ball or who had the bike last, but in the end the result is not much different from the children's as one party walks away wounded while the other never looks back. You'd think that with "maturity" we'd have learned to work out conflicts better than this, but *have* we learned?

In the end, is either party really the victor? Does the triumphant walk away *without* scars?

Isn't it true that when we hurt another human being our happiness is then chipped at as well? How can it not be?

Life is a delicate process as is happiness. Our happiness does not depend upon the actions of another person and if it did, we'd live as if on merry-go-rounds that go up and down constantly. We can't depend upon others to make us happy because most of the "others" don't know happiness any more than we do. They are seeking smiles to confirm their own identities.

We have to find solace within ourselves. We have to go beyond the day to day mundane tasks of life to see the beauty that is there. We have to search out love within the hearts of those around us and sometimes we have to work at breaking down barriers. Mostly, we have to go within and find our own peace of mind. Joy, love, happiness and contentment are there for the taking, but we have to find them within *ourselves* and it's not always easy to do this.

If we look to the external world for happiness, we will get lost in the search. We might even find it for a minute, but the reality is that it's transitory and elusive. Like a butterfly that allows us to look at it's wings as it sits on a hand for just a minute it is grace.

I am finding, however, increasingly that when I am content with who I am and what I can do with *my* life I am happy *regardless*. I have found the love within me and this has shown me the love that is there in others as well. I have found that this is true peace which *is* happiness.

When anger comes my way which it does because this is part of life and I tend to be a fiery person I have tools that help me including meditation and deep breathing. I also write in a journal and take long walks, work out in the gym, go for swims and dance in my living room as I blast my music so loud that my neighbors might complain. Let them because it's energy and in this way I release the negativity that is my anger so that I can handle conflicts calmly and rationally. This release turns me back to my heart.

I take a deep breath leaving the angry rams behind to fight their fight without me. *My* fight is for love. My fight is for peace.

I don't always win this race, but I try to especially when a friend is in trouble I try hard to be there if I can. Last night she cried. She sat on her bed with her head buried under a pillow and sobbed. I tried to comfort her. I rubbed her back and told her that she wasn't alone but she couldn't hear me. Finally, she picked up her head, looked straight into my eyes and screamed, "Leave me alone!"

I grabbed my coat and umbrella and walked into the rainy night. I squeezed my own arms against my chest and shivered. I couldn't help my friend. I walked toward my car though stood in the rain wet and unable to move. Tears commingled with rain drops.

I couldn't help her. I couldn't help myself so I stood in the rain and allowed my tears to race with lost thoughts.

My friend has lost control over her own destiny with the aid of cancer and I've lost control of my ability to help. I am speechless. I am unable to move. My brain hurts and my legs feel like led. At last, I slip into my car and drive home to an empty condo where I take a bath and fall into my bed for restless sleep. Tomorrow I will act as if nothing is wrong, but my mind will remember those I've already lost; both parents and a best friend all because of this vicious fiend called cancer.

Someone told me that it is a blessing to help another to die, but few of us surrender when it is our time to die. I'm not sure why we hang on like we do to life, to love, to friendship, etc., when these are at the end of their time. Why can't we let go when we are supposed to? There's got to be something more than this on the other side-- something more beautiful than what we *cling* to.

Life is a series of control issues. I think that this is true for most people. I am an observer. I watch people because I find them interesting.

There's a couple that I know who cling to their broken marriage. It's been a long one though perhaps too long because he cheats and she struggles to forgive. They fight, persevere and yet continue. It's painful to watch because they've loved one another, and yet, it's changed to a battle where both people attempt to control the other.

I've had controlling bosses who dictate the most minuet details. As a teacher I've had to work with my *own* issues of control within the classroom because the reality is that there is always something to have to let go of. I've worked with coworkers whose styles were different from mine. We'd clash over control issues. Over the past few years or so I finally learned that these issues are not important and that the relationship is most valuable. When I absorbed this my work relationships became easier, less stressful and much more fun.

I've known people who had control issues over drugs and alcohol. My own issue has been with food. I've had eating disorders. I felt control over my life when I *didn't* eat. Strange, huh? The feeling of being hungry reminded me that I could control my sense of need for food. Once, I became very thin; so thin that people in my life asked if I was ill and some even assumed that I was using drugs (I was not). I didn't eat because somehow the act of starving myself made me feel stronger. I've also gone in the opposite direction where I overate and put weight on as if a shield. Creating a balance and not taking my control issues out on food has and remains a struggle in my life.

Control is hard. Where do we draw the line and say I'm okay and that's enough? Try driving on a busy freeway during the commute hours and you'll see control issues at play. One person will signal to move into a different lane while another speeds up so that the signaler can't merge and then comes the honking and the middle finger is raised. Sigh...

Some people seek ways to control others through mind games and manipulative words. How can anyone feel content when struggling to control another? Think of the classic bully. What a dichotomy the need to control is because it never really gives any kind of power.

In the end, we lose that fight for control because that last breath comes when we are ready or not so I say let's get ready by finding a way to live with contentment. Our control issues only leave us striving for more which creates anxiety, frustration and anger. Who wants to live like that?

Let's let go of our need to control and go with the flow. How? Meditate. Go inward and find your greatness. The power, the sense of ease and certainty that you seek is inside you.

With the intention of 'happy' in mind I created my own ten commandments. These may not be fitting for you as they are written primarily for me. I encourage you to write your own and to live by them.

Think before you speak. This is something that I've not always been good at! Truthfully, my tendency is to put my big foot into my big mouth which has caused conflicts, but these challenges have taught me to stop and pause before speaking and make sure that it's the right time, that the person can hear it and that it's beneficial to the person so not to hurt.

Be a "Loyal" Friend and Coworker. This comes naturally to me for the most part. When my friends are in trouble I'm there for them and will go out of my way to defend them. I have given the last of my food to friends.

Take Responsibility For Your Actions. I have a Capricorn moon (nothing more needed to say) and have been shocked by how many people disregard their *own* part in conflicts. Playing the blame and shame game is not helpful to anyone and it's disrespectful of yourself. There is always a lesson to be learned for Everyone involved--never just one person...

Be Polite To Other People. You never know when you'll see the waitress at the cafe or the bus driver again and the next time that you see them they could be your boss or relative. It's a small world after all so take care of it.

Drive With Care. Take your time when driving and be careful. Too many people get into that huge ton of metal and think that it gives them the right to race around, honking and giving people the finger. Scary! Take a deep breath and drive calmly. You'll feel better and still get to your destination.

Take the Time For Personal Hygiene. I like to take a shower or a bath first thing in the morning to wash off the night and another one right before I go to bed to wash off the day. This gets me clean plus it's relaxing.

Don't Eat Animals! Love animals and don't eat them! Nuff said!

Listen With Your Heart. We're not always going to agree, but be respectful of differences and if your buttons are pushed, consider that this has to do with you and with your own perceptions.

Let Go of Anger, Hurt and Resentment. This doesn't mean that I have to include those who have been cruel to me in my life (I don't need toxicity), but holding onto injuries perceived and real only hurts me.

Take Time For Spiritual Practices. I meditate every morning and most nights before sleeping--sometimes even in the afternoons. I do Seva (selfless service) at my spiritual center a couple times a week, journal write and contemplate what comes up for me. When I do my practices I am more grounded and able to handle the challenges of my life. I also love learning about the mystical, inner journey which is light-filled, fun and beautiful!

As spiritual people we live our lives with the intention of serving humanity and with such a lofty intention you deserve to be happy! Make the space in your life for 'happy' and develop a plan of action that will help you to create whatever it is that you need to do to bring this about for you. You have the birthright to happiness within you so don't get bogged down by life's traps and trivialities. Look within you and see that you have the capability for 'happy' regardless and you deserve this gift!

Optimism In Hard Times

Her brother took her by the hand leading her as they walked from the warmth of their bedrooms and into the freezing cold morning outside as the wind blasted at her face.

Still in their pajamas both children shivered. She made a "brrrrr" sound which he ignored and instead pointed to the snow. He laughed enthusiastically and said, "Look!" His voice was eager with the thrill of newness. His name was "Optimism" and her's was "Hope." They were brother and sister and believed that together they could take on the world and isn't this like the children that we as adults teach or parent? In their amazing hearts there is nothing that is too challenging or daunting in this life that they have received. They are here with a willingness to take it *all* on and to show us adults how it's done with great enthusiasm.

It is my recollection that although, my brother's name is not "Optimism" and mine is not "Hope" this actual account of newness is one of a childhood event that happened in my life. Perhaps it is also one that you can relate to? Do you remember the days when you were a child and all that you had to face meant adventure? Do you also recall those times when a parent or teacher held you back from your challenges which left you disappointed?

It is important for us adults to help the children to retain a sense of optimism; a sense of challenge and of freedom. I love to see this within the children, and often feel that the children elicit this mindset within me despite that previously it was buried from years of non use. With the freedom that they take for granted the children show me that it is possible to have this mind set again and that is a gift.

When do we lose this sense of optimism? When do we stop looking at challenges as opportunity and start seeing them as struggles? When is it that we give up our hope and why?

I think that it is natural for human beings to embrace life head on, to take on risks and to try what is new with passion. Look at little children who are learning to walk. They don't give up after the first fall. They laugh and get up to try it all again. However, I have also noted that we lose this somewhere on the road of life and what we previously held as delightful becomes laborious. Sometimes adversity that is tossed our way changes our attitudes toward exploration. We start to believe that we can't continue, that we don't have the energy and we feel that we no longer have hope much less optimism. Growing up we are influenced by our adults rightly and/or wrongly. I say this because often it is with the best of intentions that adults rob children of the great potential within called optimism.

A former coworker had incredible heart break. Her son, a young man in his early twenties was unfairly killed. This woman knew more heartache than do most, yet, moved along with her life and I admired her greatly. I appreciated that she chose to work with children in the face of her tragedy and for the most part loved how she interacted with them.

However, maybe because of her heartache her efforts to "protect" often held the children back. She was fearful and you could see this as she scowled when the children attempted any kind of risk. It was clear that she was not an admirer of challenge. Maybe at one time in her life she was one who pushed the limits, however, as a teacher she was critical of other adults who embraced the plucky child's right to defy fear and jumped at the child to make him or her stop. She projected her own worries onto the children. I understood why she did what she did, but I also wished that she didn't do this because I saw how it not only held the child back, but also instilled a sense of fear that wasn't there before. This, however, is certainly not to say that we should not protect our children and do our best to keep them safe. Ultimately, finding that happy balance of protection and allowance of exploration is the key.

It is important for children to express bravery. This is how they learn to trust their own instincts and to believe that steadfast optimism makes them stronger.

It is in the face of fear that we create optimism which pulls us through hard times. In this way, we see challenge again as opportunity and even as adventure. We then can walk out into that cold and see the brightness that is the freshly fallen snow despite our shivering bodies. We see the grand!

However, the reality is that many of us are facing difficult times presently and this makes it hard to be optimistic.

Unemployment is almost at the rate that it was during the Great Depression, people are losing homes and people are going to bed hungry. To conquer trials we have to develop our lost optimism or we will sink along with the tides of these difficult times. We have to have courage. My grandmother used to say, "This too will pass." My grandmother was a woman who went through the Great Depression with spunk! She moved from Michigan to New York City with her two children, aging mother, sick sister and young nephew to buy a brownstone and take in tenants so that she could support her family. She often got down on her hands and knees to scrub floors, but she made it! She made a living literally. Years later as an old woman she told her young granddaughter about those times and she laughed. Her optimism proved strong and this helped her to face challenges which she later recalled with great fondness!

These are hard times for sure, but we can take on my grandmother's optimism. We can see challenges as passing and we can become steadfast in our own triumph of spirit. When we do this we regain the sense of self that we held dearly as children. We are then able to climb the mountains of hope without fear of falling. We can see to the other side and know that it is just as bright it was when we viewed it as children.

At any rate, the optimism within the child can still be honored within us adults and this will help us during these tough times. Take deep breaths and let go of fear. Do not allow fear to hinder your life. Consider instead that this just may be your calling for adventure. Be bold and courageous so that you are able to embrace the optimism of the children.

Remember that old song, "You and Me Against The World?" Does it ever feel like it's just you against the world as if your back is to the wall and there's **no** way out?

Occasionally, I feel that way and it scares me. It makes me sad and if I dwell on it, the feeling becomes oppressive.

However, I **know** that it's just a *feeling* and that feelings move on. Feelings are as transient as everything else within this world so there's little need to become attached to them. It's more important to look at them, see what is coming up and why so that you can contemplate the feelings without *indulging* in them. They pass like everything else, but they do have meanings and power behind them like the wings of the bird in flight which hold up the wind beneath that bird. Our feelings can be potent.

How do you examine your own feelings without becoming buried in them? I meditate and when I do this I pay attention to where the energy of the feeling is within my body. I can tell if that feeling is sitting in my belly roaring at me with anxiety, swirling around in my heart begging to be released or cascading in my throat wanting only to be heard. The feeling might be manifesting itself as anger and I might **want** to tell someone off, but this doesn't mean that I *should*. Think about the ramifications of allowing our emotions to run free. We'd be screaming at the mail carrier when he's late or hugging the grocery store manager because he supplied us with our favorite flavor of ice cream. People might get the wrong impressions of us, right? Ought oh!

I've often watched children work with their feelings. Sometimes these feelings overwhelm them and unlike most adults children don't have the ability that we do to censor their feelings. When angry they lash out and it's often not sweet, however, what is great about children is that they relinquish the fire of the feelings immediately after exploding. They don't carry *grudges*. They might pout and feel sorry for themselves for a minute, but it rarely lasts for long. They can be angry with a friend one minute and are holding hands the next. I love that about them because it's **wise** not to hold onto anger, sadness, worry, etc., because those kinds of emotions can swallow you--if you allow them to. These fester in your psyche and ultimately rob you are your enthusiasm.

I learn from the children. I love watching their excitement about the world. When a child sees a bird, for instance, he will often attempt to catch it while we adults rarely *notice* the bird. Children are in touch with something deep within them that is part of the Universe. This is part of all of us, but somehow we've forgotten the greatness of enjoying what is there for us.

Truthfully, the **issues** that people create rarely are important because in the end it is the heart that matters; it is love.

Remember when you were a child and you had a best friend. Remember that closeness that you shared whether it was when you explored your world or told secrets to one another you felt that it was just the two of you and that you'd always be close. It may be years since you've seen that person, and yet, somewhere in your heart that person still thrives as the *child* that you loved. Love never dies so when you feel that it is just you against the world remember that friend and remember your own boldness as a child. Remember your **enthusiasm** for life.

You and me, babe, against the world forever.

All that greatness and all that love that you once knew and even took for granted is still there in your heart as you. Let it out occasionally and most definitely show this to the children who you love. When you do this you will impress them that love is the most important ingredient to every lesson that we have to offer. It is who we are as people and one of the greatest gifts that the children have to bestow upon us is their zest for life. Take this gift in and be with it because this will help with your life. Regardless of whatever age that you are at presently you still have the love in your heart of the child and that is an amazing thing in itself so use that heart for good!

Agreements Made With God

I've had an ongoing contemplation about agreements made with God.

The agreements that I am referring to do not pertain to ambition. Perhaps God arranged for some to be doctors and others to be lawyers, but I've wondered more about how we react to our lives due to our habits.

I don't pretend to know what happens before we take birth, but I do believe in reincarnation and think that there are purposes for our lives. I've been a meditator for almost twenty years and in that time I've seen myself go through many changes especially in how I respond to the life around me. Meditation and contemplation has tweaked my way of being, however, as I progress I see more that needs to be improved upon.

People come in all shapes, sizes and colors. We also come with our own tendencies. We can be outgoing or shy for instance. Some people have fiery tempers while others hold everything in to the point where they get ulcers. Some people are extremely proud while others are humble. It's important to realize that these are qualities within the children in our lives just like they are in adults. This recognition will help us to start to see the children for who they are regardless of the glasses that we may wear as we perceive them. This allows us to let go of what we hold as important for them and permits them to be true to who they are as their own people. When we see the children for who they are we come to value their internal qualities.

When I was a young girl in school I was very shy. I would sit with a group of kids and wish that I could join in on their conversations but fear of being judged held me back. It wasn't until I was an adult that I realized that this shyness was just as egotistical as is arrogance because both tendencies have to do with the perception that people's thoughts are revolving around you. This realization was freeing for me, and yet, I still tended to hold back especially when I thought that my speaking up might cause friction. My spiritual teacher saw this in me and gave me a present one time. It was a cute little beanie baby stuffed dog and it's name was, "Spunky." I got it! She was telling me to go ahead and speak my truth. This was a gift and since that time I've rarely held back. I *am* "Spunky."

My spiritual teacher gave me a gift which transformed one of my tendencies so that my life could be improved upon; so that *I* could be improved upon.

What if before we took birth, we had a conversation with God in which we made agreements that pertained to improvements? What if during this conversation, we made a list of things that drew us to Him in greater light? This list might have included tendencies that were apparent during past life times that needed to be worked on.

In some of my meditations I've had experiences; visions and perceptions that I've thought were from former lives and these gave way to some of the tendencies that I've had during this lifetime. This gave some "aha" moments why I've responded to this life as I have.

Just for instance, say that you were a dancer in a former life and your efforts to perform required a tenacity that otherwise you may not have had. In this lifetime you may also have tenacity even if you are not a dancer. This tendency makes you a harder than average worker and gives you an extra does of determination when times are challenging in your life.

Tendencies can help and they can hurt.

What if during your conversation with God, you decided that during your last time around you were "mistrusting" and you agreed that in this lifetime you would learn to let go more, to surrender and to trust? This is just one example of a tendency that you may have made as an agreement to work on.

Presently, I see myself working on becoming more flexible with the life around me. It's not easy, but ultimately, I perceive that this will give me a greater sense of freedom. With the agreement to work on "flexibility" tests come up involving aspects of this tendency. This helps me to see if I've progressed, and to know what still needs to be worked on.

As a teacher I have had the privilege to witness what children worked on in terms habits. Their traits are not as clearly defined as adult's are, but these traits nevertheless are there. Thankfully, in children these inclinations are more mutable than what adult's are. These predispositions are not as ingrained within their systems as adult's are because the world has yet to stamp its ideals onto them. With that in mind, it has always intrigued me that when observing a child I may have impressions, for instance, that he is "Stubborn," "Willful, etc., though a week later the very quality that I labeled altered completely. Children are able to push through their predilections with productivity so that they mature and grow in this world. The stubbornness that I observed becomes a useful quality. For example, that "Willful" child will become 'determined' when attempting to learn challenging skills. He is "Perseverant" rather than "Stubborn."

I learn a great deal from children and when I see penchants that I previously considered less than desirable manifested into strengths I am always impressed. I've seen this happen repeatedly with children because they don't get bogged down by judgments that we adults often hold onto. Their inclinations, therefore, are easier to not only work with, but to transform positively repeatedly as they grow. In this way, temperamental qualities that may have been perceived negatively become purposeful in the process of maturation of the child.

Fundamentally, through this process I have come to respect that children are their own beings. By the idea of "own" I mean that they have come into this world having made agreements with God before having taken birth which may have nothing to do with us. When I came to realize this I began to recognize the child's own internal power. I've also acknowledged that they have their own karma to work on.

Often times we as adults believe that we have the duty to "mold" children into better, more responsible people, but truthfully, this process is best done when we accept the children as their *own* people. Of course, we teach social skills and hope that they learn particular morals, ethics, etc., but ultimately we need to respect who they are internally. When we come to this understanding we see the child as great regardless. We are conscious of the fact that like us they have agendas that they've created with God despite what we may hold for them. Consequentially, we come to a higher place of respecting the inner being within the child that also sparks something within us from a more profound place of learning. This profundity creates avenues for us to travel into the mind and heart of the child as a channel of God and spirit.

I once taught a little girl who was born without a particular bone in either of her forearms giving way to shorter arms than what is considered, "Normal." Before this child came into the classroom her mother met with me to discuss what she thought that Molly needed. She was of course worried that Molly would get hurt by the other children, however, she also didn't want for Molly to be held back because of a perceived "disability."

I was tentative after the meeting with Molly's mother. I didn't know exactly what to expect and only hoped that I would be able to serve this child in the best way that I could. I prepared myself to be "protective" of her. What I didn't realize at the time was that this child would come into the classroom with a tendency of resolve that was all her own. This was a girl who would not be ignored or babied. She was smaller than were the other children and her arms were shorter, but she had learned ways to use them that prompted success. She was also highly assertive and bright. However, what I was most impressed with was her distinct willingness to take on whatever it was that was thrown in her direction. This was a child who had tenacity that would never be stopped!

I saw through Molly how an innate tendency was used to accomplish difficult tasks as well as emotionally perceived barriers. Molly became a leader in the classroom. She was well loved not because anyone felt sorry for her, but because of her readiness for challenge as adventure. We saw her unwavering resolution of tenacity and we admired her for this.

Through Molly I also questioned the idea of karma. Obviously, Molly had a particular karma to be born without the bones in her forearms. However, with the propensity for determination that was displayed by Molly I wondered about the agreement that she made with God to also show others courage when faced with the *perception* of an adversity.

How about you? What are you working on during this lifetime? What do you think that you agreed on with God before you came here? Or do you think that life is all just a random crap shot of whatever happens? I think that it's more than that.

I wrote the following letter to myself~

Dear Willfulness,

Thank you for being in my life. You have surfaced many times during challenges and your strength aided me. You helped teach me not to give up and to resist temptations that may have harmed me. I am truly grateful for how you have helped me.

However, you also have held me back in many ways from going forward with my gifts and with believing in my talents. You created fear and a stubborn streak that need't be there and didn't help my life. You caused me to hold onto out dated ideas and fears that should have been let go of because if I released these things, there would be freedom, serenity and more hopefulness in my life.

I ask thereby to relinquish you with TRUST in the Universe that whatever God puts in my life is for the best and that I listen to my inner voice which guides me without being held back by you.

In doing this I ask you, Willfulness, to remember all the blessings that have come regardless of circumstances especially those that came unexpectedly. I ask you to recall the times that you felt afraid, pressured and intimidated, yet, somehow protection was ultimately assured.

Dear Willfulness, recollect the times when the outcome despite the tribulations was for the best and acknowledge this with gratitude knowing that there is something stronger than you that loves, guides, fortifies and safeguards. This remembrance gives freely with the understanding that it will be okay in the end regardless. This knowledge allows love and peace.

Thank you again for being in my life and thank you for the opportunity to surrender you to God.

Much love,

Marian

Abide in "Calm"

My journey to the spirit began in childhood. I was open and saw things that others didn't. I had visitations from spirits and angels which never frightened me. I remember my mother telling me that this was my "imagination," but I knew intrinsically that it was much more than anything that the mind could have created and with that knowledge I later decided to become a teacher. I knew somehow that I could learn through the children and that the information that I had received as a child would be expanded when with children. When a young teacher with heart in hand and an openness that lacked preconceptions I knew that there was something that the children were yet to show me. It was then that I began to see that the spirit that I knew as a child was available to me through the minds and hearts of the children. I had a strong desire to give back to the world and I knew that this longing was all that I could offer. I think that the children saw this in me unconsciously. I wasn't sure of what was needed or how the journey would unfold. The children, however, pushed me forward as if nodding me along this expedition into the world within that only they knew of. It became a mystical, magical, sometimes serene though often chaotic, but always subliminal and divinely acquired process.

When I first started teaching I was daunted by the sudden awareness that the children were huge. They were only "little" in statue and I was aware of their potential at any given moment. I was just beginning to recognize how transcendental this process of simply being around these amenable and aware people the children were. I started to see the power that they held which was far greater than what I had studied in school and this took me back to where I was as a child. I began to realize that this potential never leaves us, but we somehow forget it as life carries us through it's challenges. Still, this is the most basic aspect of being a human. It is important and it is something that all of us should find a way to reconnect to.

When with children as a teacher I was often taken to a place of deep humility. The children somehow always matched my internal state which astonished me. I was just beginning to become aware of their capabilities when they read me intuitively as if to feed off of my energy and manifest what I had unconsciously elicited. I came to know that there is no hiding with children because they sense the spirit within. They are not afraid of what should be natural though what most adults shun. I was intrigued with what I intuited in the consciousness of the child immediately with a sense that this connection of spirit was what I wanted and was what they took for granted.

The children then became great mentors and as I have progressed I have been fortunate to have the acquisition of both spiritual and worldly teachers to further learn from.

As a young teacher I met a man who taught me skills needed in a classroom though these assets went well beyond and into the school of the world. He showed me the importance of the energy within the classroom which is the essential part of the world that allows for the give and take of spirit to take place with ease. This force is that of the Universe and is within everyone. It guides us when we listen to it. With this non-limiting vitality we are protected due to the profundity of the directions that we receive when we tune into this energetic field. It is the spirit within all and is where the highest teaching occurs.

This man was a joyful person though extremely calm and respectful of each child and where that child was as a person. This respect is crucial because without this quality we are unable to reach *any* other person's greatest capacity and we then become unheard and unseen. This inward connection to spirit of adult and child and is between any people becomes a mutual exchange of resources through respect and love. It is an invisible motion that is permeated into every aspect of how information is taught and perceived. However, this energy is continuously changed as it transmutes information from and to each person.

I noticed when with this particular person that the children listened to him. As a teacher he imparted an air of authority and I was impressed. I wanted what he had because then I often went home quashed and run over by my students. Contrarily, he was able to elicit listening from the child's higher perceptions which drew forth knowledge and understanding. I knew intuitively that this gift of active listening is what all people strive to be given.

I watched because he appeared easy going, yet, had complete control over the entire group. I recognized that his deep, male voice elicited command. Obviously, as a young female there was no way that I could ascertain this feature though I observed a "Singsong" quality in his voice which I too could use. This resonated with depth at times, softness at others and with high tones during different times. I noted how this attracted the children's attention and helped to create a sense of melodic balance in the classroom. I saw then how this vocal quality had an attention grabber within the world and began to know that this is the song of the soul.

This Singsong quality within the voice was dynamic as it came from a deeper place than the mind. It reverberates from a high vibration and allows the spirit to come through with openness and this quality alters the capacity for exuberance as well as the potential for greatness. This became apparent to me as fluid, transparent and extremely powerful.

This teacher also used play to demonstrate ways to learn. The children appeared more eager to engage in the tools that were presented and to participate with an equal amount of enthusiasm shown to them when play was used as an instrument to learning. At times, he was even silly which broke monotony and further elicited interest. However, calmness always permeated throughout the classroom. It was again a vibration that executed advancement and would effectuate the ability to transform challenges into tools for learning.

I saw that the use of play and even silliness could revamp provocations and motivate the children. It then occurred to me that we as adults also absorb information with ease when we are joyful.

I saw too a listening ability that came from a deep place of quietude. This listening was demonstrated with affection, open hearted questions and with silence.

I learned then that the gift of silence often says much more than words can. It gives a space to be heard and cared for in a deeper sense than chatter allows. This space invites each of us into a place of the heart where communication happens telepathically as well as allows us the voice of our own intuition. It becomes a union of soul matter.

Working with children has taught me a great deal about who we are as spirits because of the child's lack of hesitation for what we have become afraid to acknowledge. They jump into the waters of life regardless of perceived sharks and ride with the tides enthusiastically.

Attachments and Boundaries

Children are highly sensitive. They sense our fears and needs and extract this. This is why it is said that children know how to push adults' buttons.

When I first became a teacher with young children an overwhelming abundance of love flowed, however, this was like a drug. Instead of illuminating it was addictive and fed the ego because this "love" created attachment.

Insecure with myself I sought evaluation from the children in my life as if their love fed a need for worthiness within me. This absorption, however, devalued my internal strength as a person because it was an egoistic desire for validation of the self as the role that I played as "teacher." As I held onto this unhealthy aspiration I became attached to a child who I perceived had "needs" for attention. Literally, we energetically matched one anther and this created a vicious cycle which I justified because the child was undergoing trauma from his parents' nasty divorce. This prompted me to give him extra affection, praise, smiles and hugs which he lapped up and begged for more. I literally *babied* him, and he, in turn, latched onto me.

Supervisors told me that this was not only inappropriate, but also not beneficial for the child because it did not offer skills that would help him to contend with difficulties.

What I did not realize at the time is that children have their own karma and even when we love them we cannot change this. I came to see the value of helping a child to take on his life with courage and that this imparts a skill that is more beneficial for that child's life than it is to coddle him. Courage, after all, will remain with that child throughout his life to assist him with challenges while coddling only helps during fluctuating moments. Ultimately, coddling does not have the power that courage has to transcend life's difficulties.

In dealing with this family in crisis I also learned the importance of compassionate boundaries. This taught me to let go of my need for validation because it got in the way of a sincere offer to help. When I surrendered this ego need for acceptance I was able to simply be who I was as a person with children and with other people in my life. It was only then that I could offer from the heart because then I was able to sincerely show the truth of me to other people.

Years later, as with the cycle of life, I saw how this played out again when another teacher in a classroom that I taught also babied the children. I clearly recognized her need for validation as one that I had once also stubbornly held onto. This neediness triggered a behavior that undermined the children's potential for growth as well as their ability to tune into their highest Selves. I talked to her about this which went over like a led balloon.

I came to believe that like the children adults also go through unconscious stages of development. Ironically, however, when we fail to see the greatness of the child or of any other person we hinder that person's spiritual development as this prevents exploration of Self. This may be why we stopped progressing spiritually when we were children. The adults in our lives saw to it that our inner wisdom was curtailed instead of nurtured because of their own fears. I began to acknowledge how in the progression of the spirit there becomes an understanding of the importance for *detached* love. This detachment creates a holistic expansion of manifestation into wholeness which cannot happen when another person's energy is excessively intrusive within our space.

I came to learn that when we are balanced detached love comes easily. It is then that we are able to give compassion and affection without forming negative attachments. This creates freedom for other people in our lives to be true to who they are. Detached love also forms soul connections that are much deeper than are relationships which are based on needs for validation as this need comes from the ego and not from the heart.

With a lack of attachment we are able to create a true formation of love where bonds are created with freedom for exploration. These connections promote growth intrinsically which further allows for a flow of a higher vibration toward betterment. This currency draws flexibility and autonomy within children and for the people in our lives who we love.

Paradoxically, when we give detached love our confidence in our highest Selves also increases because like the child who is free to reach a higher state we also come to sense that internal liberation. This is so basic, and yet, an advanced state of teaching and learning for all of us and with this there comes a greater connection of joy. This communion with our higher possibilities is a recognition of what we knew intuitively as children through detached love, non-judgment and trust.

Boundaries

When I first started teaching it amazed me when old memories were triggered from my own childhood through my work with children. It was as if seeing my childhood traumas being played out in front of me again. I think that this happens as we all progress through life. We look back at what happened to and with us as if watching a movie and hopefully we learn through this.

Working with children, however, was powerful spiritually for me because these memories which are often unresolved issues came up for contemplation, meditation and healing. I often saw myself through the children and was reminded of things that I had forgotten or had unconsciously completely buried. This purposeful synchronistic quality edged me toward spiritual growth which was profound because it elicited childhood traumas for resolution.

This often felt as if living in a parallel life that was played out in front of me twenty or more years after the occurrences had happened within my own life. It was profoundly healing, but I also had to learn how to use these memories most effectively for myself as well as for those around me. For instance, can you imagine a simple a memory of when your mother forgot to pick you up after school and left you stranded in the rain for hours? You've forgotten about this time in your life until the day when little Joey is also left standing to wait for his mom whose time has escaped her. Your heart goes out to Joey, but because of your own heart break his experience feels immensely resonant as if your own experience. This elicits anger and when you finally see Joey's mother you give her hell. Sound familiar? This is just one example of how memories are jogged and can be played out through the children.

Memories are often exaggerated so that they are extracted, resolved and eventually healed. However, I also found that if we are not conscious of how we go about this healing process we can do damage to the psyches of the children who we are attempting to protect. This havoc occurs when we forget to be mindful of how to process our information so that it does not extend negatively into the children's experiences for their own lives.

I had to learn to use good boundaries and be mindful of what was mine and what was the other person's. Processing painful memories is not easy especially when we see similar things that once happened to us with the children in our present lives. We want the best for the children and we don't want for them to have to undergo the kinds of painful experiences that we went through, however, we must remember that these are also potential lessons which we also don't want to rob the children of. We have to remind ourselves that each person is here on this plane of learning for their own purposes and that each individual has his or her own karma which has nothing to do with us. The karma that we share with the children in our lives is transcendental and should promote evolution. This is an interweaving of love for all humanity that permeates into the world.

When boundaries are not observed, however, it becomes easy to forge our own life lessons onto the children which ultimately should have nothing to do with these children and can be more harmful than beneficial. This is the ultimate in ego. I once taught with a woman who constantly spoke about her childhood as if her's and the children's were the same. Her psychological and psychic buttons were often triggered which caused her to expend time talking about how her experiences negatively effected her life. She then related these negativities to the children in a way that manipulated and controlled them. For instance, when a child was reminded of a classroom rule the teacher's emotionality was jogged because of a time when she felt punished by her parent unjustly. Still holding onto the pain of what she perceived as "unfair" she harbored animosity for authority figures especially when rules were administered. This made it almost impossible for her to set rules within the classroom or to uphold other teacher's standards of discipline which then created a chaotic classroom that had no boundaries.

It takes a great deal of internal work to be a successful person in this world spiritually.

Essentially, our scars should help us to become more compassionate and take us to that deep place of the heart where true communion takes place. This happens when we go beyond our egoistic need to control other people and the circumstances in our lives. When we allow the memories to come up, see them for what they are with dispassion healing is promoted. We are then able to have empathy for other people in a more honest manner. We are then able to relinquish our scars from our past and connect with the spirit with wholeness.

The memories elicited are to be healed and this is powerful. They serve us so that we can go deeper to that place of the heart within every being on this planet and this offers understanding from a profound place because it teaches us about compassion. Ironically, when connected to the heart we are able to use our memories to help other people by remaining present oriented. This makes it easy for us to reach into our intuition for guidance within any given moment and any given occurrence. In my experience, the best possible way to do this is through meditation which keeps us grounded and heals the wounds of the past so that we do not inflict them onto those within our present time. We, instead are able to use these experiences for the greater good because we have the detachment needed to see clearer.

Meditation is an amazing tool because it is grounding, calming, healing and promotes internal growth. It also helps to heal past memories and creates boundaries so that these memories remain our own without any infliction onto other people. Through meditation we are able to witness the memories from the past with a lack of emotionality so that we can work through them and heal them. When we use tools like meditation our living process becomes therapeutic for ourselves and for everyone in our lives.

We begin then to remember that our childhoods are ours to honor. With this we also have the conviction to bless the childhoods of the people who we care for with positivity and love.

Daily meditation benefits our actions throughout our days because it carries a higher vibration. The best times to meditate are before dawn and when we meditate at the same time and in the same place daily our meditations are most powerful.

Meditation

I used to live in a state of moon beams and rainbows or nightmarish howls and cries. I lived on ups and downs. This scenario created either exuberant highs or extreme lows with little in between. I called myself, "Sensitive" and still tend to have bouts of the "Worrier" rather than "Warrior."

However, meditation has helped me. It keeps me calm during tribulations, grounds me and helps me to be more attune with other people.

People think of meditation as a way to calm the body, but it does much more. Meditation forces the practitioner to contemplate his or her habits that create unhappiness for that person. Habits, therefore, are examined so that changes can be made toward improvement.

At first, I was particular about where and how I meditated. I created a lovely spot with pillows, candles, incense and pictures. I wore all white and kept this area spotlessly clean. However, meditation can be done anywhere. I still have a special area in my home to meditate, but love to sit and meditate on a rock by the Bay where I live or even in my car during breaks at work.

Meditation elicits visions and insights which should be contemplated because they are from the divine. When something occurs during meditation the seeker should know that this is not a random thought. This is from God. It's a message which needs to be received with reverence. After I meditate I often journal about my meditation experience. This helps me to remember the experience and takes me deeper to that place of knowingness and insight. This process helps me to contemplate profoundly. In addition, there is energy in writing.

Another huge tool that comes from meditation is detachment. I once worked in a toxic environment where the majority of the people complained and backstabbed. While there I became physically ill. I had pneumonia and even chicken pox. I was exhausted physically and emotionally from the many sparring matches and one day it occurred to me that detachment eased the daily drama of the environment, and helped to overcome its effects.

I made a conscious effort to become detached and even told this to my coworkers who balked that this would make me, "Cold." The reality is that I've never been a "Cold" person in my life and detachment doesn't equal "Cold."

When detached we disentangle from other people's garbage and we take responsibility for our own authenticity. When detached we become real and don't allow others to disrupt our internal state. This process creates boundaries. When I practiced this my coworkers were surprised because I was no longer reactive. I was, however, smiling. My relationships in this otherwise still toxic environment changed, and in turn, I forgot about the perniciousness. I let go of negativity and instead saw positivity in those around me although they hadn't changed at all.

'I' had changed and this elicited a realm of happiness regardless.

Meditate for joy, health and for serenity. It will change your life for the better and it will most definitely help you to be the best person that you are capable of being!

When you meditate you become aware of the inner world as well as the world around you. It is a healing process that extends energetically into the world and this has a profound effect on people, animals and on our environment.

Consider that in this present time which is thought of as the period of darkness and known in the East as "Kali Yuga" or "the age of vice" many people are currently wakening to the inner spirit through the process of meditation. This raises vibrations and heals the world as we know it.

It is said that during the epoch "Kali Yuga" people are far removed from God and this equates behaviors that some may refer to as "evil." It's a time of destruction that predetermines where and what we are due to the consequences of our past actions. However, even though the world at present can feel challenging, scary and not welcoming there *is* a **healing** force which is driven through the power of meditation.

This force known as "Kundalini" is tremendous, powerful and incredible. It is a restorative force that drives into deep lifetimes of scars to elicit painful experiences to be freed from the psyche. *This* is not like an earthly experience. When I see birds in flight I am reminded of the great Kundalini that gives way to freedom so that I too can soar. It spins, swirls and thrusts our power to God to draw out our divinity.

The Kundalini is extremely powerful. It is an "intelligent" energy that knows what to do so that you can handle the information that it brings forth. For example, there may be memories from this lifetime or from others that you have buried and can't recall because they are too painful. These memories *will* come up, but *only* when you are *ready* and **strong** enough to work on them. The Kundalini prepares you and makes you stronger.

After a while of doing this internal work through meditation, contemplation, selfless service, chanting, prayer and journal writing you become able to see patterns occur and you will see this in the way that you go about your work in the world and well as how you interact with other people. You will also find yourself more in awe of the children in your life as vibrant beings and you will come to know who they are as spiritual beings because children tune into the spirit with ease. Your habits which are your routines, addictions and ways of being which create obstacles in your life will also be seen clearly. When you continue doing this work you will be able with the grace of a Master (teacher, Guru, guide) to make needed changes for self improvement toward a better and more joyful life.

As you progress synchronicity develops and creates "Aha" moments that reveal to you why *this* occurred and became *that*. You will also begin to notice how past intuitions showed you what may be happening in your life presently.

As you continue your progression you will begin to recognize your own greatness and know that you are connected to a higher source within. You will also recognize that this connection is part of the Universe and ties all of us together as One.

In a world that can be seen as "evil" it is miraculous to meditate and find Godliness in the your Self and in that of humanity. Meditate to see the highest in yourself, the children in your life, adults who you care for and even those who you've never met.

Here are some recommendations:

Books by my spiritual Master, Gurumayi Chidvilasanda:

Sadhana Of The Heart, The Yoga of Discipline, Enthusiasm, Remembrance, My Lord Loves A Pure Heart, Inner Treasures and The Magic of the Heart

There are many CDs available including Meditation Instructions led by Gurumayi and of the mantra, "Om Namah Shivaya."

You can find all of these here~

http://siddhayogabookstore.org

The child saw the matches sitting on the table and remembered the vibrant and luscious fire that was produced by his mother when she used these to light her cigarette. It was so glorious; in fact, that he wished that he could reach out and touch those crimson flames within his small hands.

He licked his lips and took out a match. He stared at it knowing that it could create something glorious and with that he struck the match across the black part of the container just as he had seen his mother do. Immediately, before his very eyes flashed an orange, gold, red and blue flame! He was mesmerized by its splendor and stared into it when his mother screamed, "NO!"

Startled the child dropped the flame onto the coffee table while his heart beat so loudly that he could almost hear it. His mother grabbed a nearby flower vase and threw water from it onto the flames drenching out the hot magnificence. That night the child received the only spanking that he had ever had and cried not due to physical pain, but because an illusion of grandeur had been put out.

Across town a young woman stared into a full length mirror. At sixteen, she was more woman than girl and her beauty was vibrant. She stared into the mirror and into the green, gold eyes that reflected back at her. With a flick of a hand she threw her yellow curls over her shoulders and watched in the mirror as they cascaded around her face. She stared into the reflection that paralleled back at her and began to undress peeling off her tight sweater and throwing it onto the floor to examine the shape of her breasts pictured in front of her. They were ripe, full and upright. She took her hand and touched one caressing it before slipping out of her skirt. She then stood naked in front of the mirror and watched her body move with her thoughts. Her young woman's body felt new to her as just a year ago her breasts were as flat as were her younger brother's. She smiled and at the same time felt scared by her own apparent sensuality.

What she didn't see in that mirror were her neighbor's watchful eyes. From his bedroom he sat at his own window where he peered into her bathroom. This sixty-five year old man sat at his window and smiled as he watched his young female neighbor peel off her clothes in front of her mirror. He grinned as if she was there just for his entertainment.

Downstairs from where he sat his wife also sat. In her worn lazy boy chair she looked at old photographs from days long gone. There in these faded pictures stood a girl with a breathtakingly beautiful smile. The woman in the lazy boy chair touched the face in the photograph as tears welled up in her eyes. She cried for the illusion of her lost beauty. She also cried because her husband no longer looked at her the way that he now looks at her sixteen year old neighbor.

Interrupted by a jolt the woman answered her telephone to hear her oldest friend's voice shrill from weeping. The voice cried that her husband had lost his battle with cancer. She said that her life would never be the same and that his was all that she had lived for. She whispered that she wished that she could just see his face one last time.

A few miles away another woman was being driven in a taxi to a hospital. She was pregnant and was about to give birth. She cried, "Drive faster!" The taxi driver drove as fast as he could, but the baby was impatient to be born. The driver pulled to the side of the road while calling 911. He helped the woman in the backseat with his awkward hands and breathed in and out relief when at last the cry of life was heard. The last time that he had witnessed a birth was when his own wife delivered an infant though his was stillborn. Now, he held this tiny new life in his arms and sighed.

At the same time, another man sat in a meditation hall deep within his own center of consciousness. In this profound inner space the man entered a tunnel of blue light. There in that tunnel of blue stood divine spirits. A voice began to speak and told the man that his "reality" is not his work place, his home or even his body. The voice continued to say that what was witnessed in meditation is the only reality. With that the divine spirit faded and the man's meditation continued with a white star that unfolded into thousands of greater and more brilliant lights that broke open with heat that was almost unbearable. The man at last opened his eyes. Sweat poured from his brow. He knew that he had experienced his own greatest Self. He had seen what is real, impermeable and the infinite.

It is said in The Upanishads, "There are two selves, the apparent self and the real Self. Of these it is the real Self, and he alone, who must be felt as truly existing. To the man who has felt him as truly existing he reveals his innermost nature." The man in the meditation saw this. All the others in this essay saw only illusions of what is real. They saw what will only fade away while the man that meditated saw what has always been and what will always be.

He saw God.

Guided By Intuition

These are difficult times with jobs and many people are struggling to find employment. Consider that there are four people for every one position available currently and with that we know that a good resume is helpful for any career's purpose, however, in today's economy we need more than this. It's great to know what are the latest theories for our chosen professions so that we are up to date and current with today's economy.

It's also beneficial to throw ideas back and forth with coworkers as to gain insights and explore avenues of approach. Ultimately, during these challenging times many people disregard that little voice within which indicates what directions to take. This is our intuition and is a basic innate quality that we should all rely on. It is our antenna that reaches from our hearts to other people's and back again. It is how children communicate naturally.

While working with children I've seen that the best teachers know that a good education is absolutely necessary and that the ability to tune into the intuition is also required. There needs to be both the outside learning from the classroom as well as the guidance from that inner voice called, "Intuition." Listening to your intuition will aways steer you in the right direction and I think that this is valid for any career choice.

Truthfully, when I took my classes in education one of the reasons why I knew that this was the right field for me was that it not only came easily but as common sense. I knew that the information that I learned was already within me and that I needed to tune into it. What the books described only validated what I already knew in my heart. This internal knowledge supplied me with easy "A's" as well as the ability to have fun with my classes. I thoroughly enjoyed them because I felt intuitively attuned with what I was taught. Contrarily, I've taken courses in the past that did not resonate with me and therefore struggled with them. In my opinion, when this happens it is a sign that this may not be the right direction to take career wise. Your career should speak to your heart intuitively just like everything else in your life should. If this is not the case, you might need to make changes as you will continuously be discontent as well as more than likely less successful than you would in a field that feeds your heart. Your career ultimately should allot for an ability for you to use your own internal instincts and intuition.

The first time that I got to use my internal resources with my studies came during an internship. I worked in a Kindergarten classroom with a teacher, an aide and thirty children. It was a busy classroom filled with activities that kept the children occupied, but there was one little girl who couldn't seem to get with the program. She stayed to the sides with a thumb in her mouth and tears in her eyes unnoticed because she was often silent except for the sounds of quiet crying. She appeared not to want to be seen and to be afraid.

Perhaps because I had been a shy child myself I related to little Susanna. Remember the chapter about how our memories can either serve us while with children or hinder us? The memories that came up for me were similar to what I observed in Susanna. I remembered myself standing by the sidelines with tears in my eyes and hopes that no one noticed until I could go home. I remembered and I felt sad. I felt what Susanna was feeling, but my goal was not to become overwhelmed in my *own* depth of sorrow. My intention was to help Susanna to overcome her despair and become comfortable within the classroom setting.

How did I achieve this goal? I listened to my intuition which guided me to what I felt in my heart that Susanna needed.

There was an element of fear that I had to overcome because I didn't want for her to withdraw further when I approached her so was respectfully cautious. I watched when the teacher called her name to join the other children which only resulted in Susanna looking downward silently. Intuitively, I knew that she needed to trust one person at a time before she could join the entire group comfortably.

However, the teacher in charge appeared to want to create an atmosphere for the classroom rather than for the needs of the individuals. We cannot treat our children as if herds of cattle. Every child has specific needs that we as adults need to detect through conscious intention. For me as a teacher I knew that the effort that it took me to help Susanna would benefit each child as well as the group.

In Susanna's case she needed to learn to trust that she was safe before comfortable within the classroom environment. With this in mind, I listened to my intuition which guided me to when to approach her and when to give her space because both were needed at different times. I also was shown inwardly 'how' to approach this particular child so that she would accept my offerings and not rebuke them.

I experimented with my intuition listening to what I felt it showed me and before long Susanna was smiling. This once silent child was now talking in full sentences. She wanted to tell me her feelings, discuss her home life and what was going on within her. I listened carefully to her and to my heart and before long Susanna felt heard enough to branch out to the group. The reality was that it didn't take long for Susanna to relinquish her fears and join the classroom once she trusted the process.

In a short time, I observed this little girl who once stood back with tears smiling, laughing and playing with other children as if never afraid.

I learned through Susanna that my intuition was my best guide as a teacher. I knew then that when I listened to that little voice within me that I would be able to hear the needs of each individual child in my classroom. As I progressed spiritually I also found that this same voice could guide me with any and every person that came into my life. It's a magical, mystical process and it's fun when we pay attention to what is directly within us!

As a teacher my intuition has helped me with children consistently. I've experienced many times when children displayed frustrations, anger, sadness, etc., and when I listened to that little voice within I always knew what was the right approach needed to help each child.

Still, I've seen teachers and parents become 'automatic' with children which is how they are also with other people in their lives because they either are not aware intuitively of soul connections or they disregard them. They see a child crying, for instance, and want to help, but instead of tuning into the beacon within the teacher does what she or he has learned from a text book. In doing this, the teacher disregards the voice within which is there to guide them intuitively and instead acts in a robotic method from a text book. What works for Tim does not for Sara, but when we tune into each child we 'know' the best approach. We do this throughout our lives as we interact solely using superficial levels with those around us instead heart connections.

Intuition can make the most challenging situations easy.

In the beginning of a year in one classroom several children showed difficulties with transitioning. It was hard and headache producing as the children screamed and cried. Still, I knew how to handle each child's transition. How? Intuition.

My coworker, however, struggled with this idea. There was one child in particular who not just cried but screamed and my coworker's solution was to carry him around the classroom to quiet him. I watched her and observed him intuitively. I sensed his **strong** spirit.

After observing her with him for a while I noted that her intention was to create a soothing bond, but with this particular child this did not work as he needed validation of his anger. I suggested to my coworker to give him a particular space within the classroom where he could scream and then leave him alone. This made it acceptable in his mind to scream yet did not reinforce the negative behavior. It gave him the space to be angry though also showed him that we were not going to play into the anger. Together we designed a comfortable area within the classroom that would be his "Screaming Spot" and every time he screamed instead of picking him up my coworker led him to this area making sure that he knew that this was not a punishment, but an appropriate place for him to scream. From then on every time that he screamed she sweetly smiled and told him that he could do so as loudly as he wanted within this space only and walked away from him.

At first, it was hard for her because he continued to not only scream, but run back to her because by then he was accustomed to what reinforced the behavior: being carried around. It was challenging, but she continued the process of leading him to his "Screaming spot" without giving the behavior attention. She'd sit him down and sweetly tell him that he could scream as loudly as he wanted to but *only* in this area. She also reminded him that when he finished screaming he could join her and the other children with the "Fun" classroom activities.

She did this several times and to her surprise it didn't take long for this child to stop screaming and to join the group enthusiastically. In the process, this child found his resilience because ultimately he had a vibrant personality. In the end, this particular child became a classroom leader. He learned to direct what previously came across as demanding in a positive way that benefited him as well as the entire group. This amazing lesson would never have happened if the teacher had continued to carry him and this came about through the power of intuitively tuning into the child's real needs rather than using a superficial bandaid which ultimately did not benefit him.

Regardless if you are working with children, adults or with animals never underestimate the power of your intuition because it will help you even with the most difficult situations. You will find that when you do this internal work life will be easier for you and will be much more fun.

Haven't you had experiences of a 'knowingness' that something was not right or was even the "perfect" thing? This may have happened in a relationship with someone who you just met, yet, knew immediately that this would be someone important in your life. I think that this is common because of the karma that we share from previous lifetimes. Once while walking with a friend I saw a man who was working with children. My friend became enthusiastic about the cuteness of the children, but my eyes were drawn to the man's and his to mine. It felt like an instant connection of the soul. I didn't see him again for a few years though life brought us back together and he became someone who I have loved probably more intensely than anyone other than my spiritual teacher in this lifetime yet.

How about times when you 'felt' that this was not the time to go out though did and something happened. I remember having had this sensation though ignored it to go out with friends. That night I was in a bad car accident.

Whether your intuition shouts at you or whispers it is your guide and you should make a point to listen to it because it will keep you safer and happier.

The Offering Of Discipline

I learned a great deal about discipline for myself as a spiritual person while working with children. The word "Discipline" conjures up horror stories and scary movies, but did you know that its roots comes from the Latin word "Discere" as discipleship? A "Disciple" is a student and "Discere" means to learn.

In my life, discipline has helped me to create schedules that I stick to, get things done, and motivate me. It is purposeful in my life and makes me a better person.

However, with children discipline is often either over or under used by teachers and parents and gets a bad rap, but essentially when used to its best advantage discipline is a learning tool. Discipline creates boundaries in an otherwise large and sometimes frightening world with the intention to make children feel safer. Children need limits and will often unconsciously act out for adults to step up and set these limits which ultimately create calmness for the child.

Children want to feel protected and this is the job of discipline when used correctly. It should never be scary, threatening or imposing and it should also never be lacking.

I saw the effects of what happens when discipline is disregarded when I visited a school that didn't use any form of discipline. The philosophy of the administration didn't believe in any form of discipline and as a result teachers did not stay at this school because they often felt overwhelmed when the children acted out which they did regularly. While I was at this school I witnessed children biting, hitting, throwing heavy blocks, disrupting the classroom and not listening to the teacher's directions. In essence, this was a chaotic environment which felt unsafe for the children as well as for the adults. Truthfully, I couldn't wait to leave this campus because spiritually it felt so heavy.

Still, while at this school I spent time just hanging out with the children. At one point, the teacher attempted to give a lesson which few children paid attention to. Instead they ran around, screamed and threw things. The exasperated teacher asked me to help her with two of the boys who ignored her directions to come to circle and instead wrestled in a corner. I walked over to where the boys wrestled with large pillows which they continued to throw at one another. Initially, I sweetly asked the boys to join the teacher and they ignored my request. When I realized that this approach would not work I knew that some form of consequence was being asked of me because the children wanted for the adults to do something that made them feel safer. With this in mind, I took the pillows away from the boys and to my surprise they began to help me! They picked up the remaining pillows to hand to me in a calm fashion which was a completely different tone than what was demonstrated when they wrestled. This told me that they appreciated being given a consequence as it demonstrated to them that an adult was there for them to care for them. The boys immediately calmed down and I was able to sit with them to give them a lesson. From that point on the boys were very concentrative.

Children want discipline. It makes them feel safer. Ultimately, the purpose of discipline is to make all of us feel safer. Imagine a life with no rules or regulations. For instance, what would happen if we didn't have the police? Who would you call in the middle of the night when your neighbor got rowdy or worse? The reality is that even if you never have to make such a phone call, it makes you feel safer to know that there is someone there to protect you and your needs.

Discipline also creates a sense of order which makes us feel at ease. We as adults often check our watches because we like to know the time of the day so that we can create a schedule. Children may not be able to tell time, but they appreciate knowing what to expect and when because this elicit a sense of security.

Maria Montessori taught that there are four specific types of order to which a child is sensitive and in these sensitive periods the child is most "learning absorbent." During these periods children seek order to acclimate to the environment. She stated that younger children learn to distinguish a separation of self and environment through order. This formation of discipline occurs when the child feels that things in the classroom have a specific place, actions have consequences and that the day runs in an orderly fashion. The child feels safer because he comes to rely on this and this orderly discipline creates a sense of trust for and within the child.

While teaching I have observed that when the classroom is kept in an orderly way the children notice what is in the room and take care of it better themselves. They take on a sense of ownership of the classroom. This helps to promote internal discipline which will ultimately benefit their entire lives. Consider that through discipline the child learns to clean up after himself, stop eating when no longer hungry and to examine his own feelings. They learn that there are beginnings, middles and endings to everything. Through discipline they learn about relationships. This is essential so that the child can come to learn about him or herself as well as the world.

As teachers, parents and friends of the child it is not our responsibility to dictate. We instead want to give them the structure of discipline so that they take this in internally and make it their own. In this way, the child is able to formulate a connection with him or herself which will later help to shape his or her sense of purpose for being on this Earth plane. As a teacher, I intended to be a guide, and with this in mind, the discipline that I offered was meant to help the child to unfold so to ultimately create and manifest his life as he matured. My intention was to offer discipline in the most positive way so to be a great gift to the child and to the world in which that child will serve at large as he grows and matures.

As I worked with children and with myself I found that it was necessary to be mindful of just how to administer discipline. For instance, it is important to be consistent and to carry out discipline in a way that a child can fully understand or there is no point to it. A child must be able to connect the consequence with the action and no action is so great that the discipline should humiliate, physically or emotionally hurt or feel threatening. Discipline should never be punishing and should always be a learning tool.

It can be challenging, however, when we care for children whose cultural mores are unlike what we may hold as "ethical." This often comes to play, for instance, when children are spanked. As a teacher, of course, I would never spank a child in my classroom as this is not only in my opinion unethical, but it is also illegal for a teacher to do. The parent, however, may need to consider how this type of discipline teaches and reinforces ethics? It is my personal stance that is humiliating because it hurts physically as well as emotionally. It belittles the person who the child is and teaches the child not to trust the adult. Further, this form of discipline admonishes that the child should hit when angry. As a teacher, I have noted that those children who are spanked at home are often the hardest to discipline at school because they have been taught not to listen. This form of discipline has created a method so that simple directions are often disregarded by the child who needs firmer discipline than talking allows for. Furthermore, and maybe what is more important, they are not shown respect so why in turn should they respect other people? This is something to contemplate. Still, as a teacher I had to come to the realization that my job was to remain open minded to other cultures with differing values including those that I struggled with. This is expanding spiritually because it teaches compassion when differences arise. It teaches the importance of unconditional love versus judgment. For instance, I have had to come to accept certain situations that I had no control over with parents and other teachers and when I did this I came to love regardless. This is ultimately freeing because it takes the seeker to the realization that you don't have to change other people. You can come to accept them for who they are even if they do things very differently than you do.

While undergoing this particular challenge as a spiritual person my intention became to delve deeper to the child's essence.

Once while working with children at risk whose parents were mostly drug addicted I had the opportunity to observe children who were disciplined through spanking, yelling, etc., and as a result often these were extremely tough children. They had already been through the worst that the world had to offer and their hearts 'appeared' hardened. Intuitively, I knew that this was a facade. These were children who needed nurturance and that this would help them to open up to who they were as spiritual beings.

The harsh discipline that these children experienced made me think deeply about what type of discipline that I was to offer when it came to consequences. I knew that the children required structure and order in the classroom so that they felt safe. I knew that they also needed to be taught what was appropriate with behaviors socially. I knew these things all the while still wanting to elicit the children's internal sense of self and greatness. For me as a teacher this became about balance.

It was clear to me that the children strove to be given a sense of nurturance with appropriate boundaries that helped to bring the world in so that they ultimately felt safer. In doing this, the discipline tools that were incorporated included helping the child to sense his or her own breath, calming the child by counting his or her own fingers and with paying attention to the environment. The children learned through these things that they were in the world which they also had the power to affect. They learned that they had power that could be used for good. Isn't this ultimately what we want discipline to teach? We want for the children to acknowledge that they ultimately have a role and purpose in this world.

The challenge as a spiritual person is to determine what is the best route of discipline needed in any given situation and sometimes this takes experimentation because what works in one circumstance may not work in another. When we tune into our intuition and try different methods we can determine ways and be guides for individuals with the intention that they connect to their own internal sense of discipline. In this way, we as spiritual adults help our children to come to learn of their own capabilities.

I remember working with a particular child who was frustrating because it felt that every discipline attempt that I offered landed flat. I worked with his parents who reported to me that they also had challenges because he was stubborn and aggressive. Still, often it is this type of child that we as spiritual people learn the most from. Like challenging adults, these children become our teachers because they offer us difficult challenges to learn from. We come to recognize that they have an internal compass which defies how we attempt to direct them, and in the end, we often relinquish what we set out to do in the beginning. We surrender not to the child's frustration, but to his internal being that we come to trust in regardless because spiritually we know that each child is guided by a higher force.

It's not always easy to know how or what to do when it comes to discipline and those who tell you otherwise are not truthful. However, I firmly hold that when we as spiritual people meditate on our own greatness we come to see the potential in the children and when we have this recognition the challenges are positive ones. We learn to trust in the discipline that we offer even when it doesn't work as we planned because it has come from our hearts and we know too that it is mutable.

Ultimately, what I learned the most about discipline while teaching is that it is an intrinsic force which guides our lives toward betterment. With discipline, for instance, I am guided to wake up at dawn to do my meditations. Discipline creates an avenue for me to live my life in a way that offers routine that helps me to get things done. This structure has value for me because like the children who strive in order we also come to feel efficient in this way. This kind of discipline becomes something that I yearn for and like the children makes me feel safer. Consider that without an internal sense of discipline our lives would be chaotic. Ultimately, discipline is a fundamental gift that comes from within.

Different Styles of Learning

The other day I overheard someone talking about his friend's child. Apparently, the boy is now in middle school though has had a bumpy educational life and has often gotten into trouble. This boy has recently been placed in a more "progressive" school and is doing better, but my friend said, "I don't know what kind of career that he will ever have because he's such a *different* kind of learner..."

This sad statement got me thinking because I've spent almost all of my adult years as a teacher working with many "*different* kinds of learners." Truthfully, I've found the more challenging student was often the most endearing to me in many ways. I felt spiritually connected to these kinds of children as their struggles were seen as opportunities that yielded the heart. Yet, of course, I also felt an equal sense of awe when with the gifted child who excelled seemingly easily.

One year there was a little girl named Emma who was a child that excelled. She came into the classroom with an obvious determination that held on like spunk regardless of what challenge that she was up against. I couldn't help but laugh when Emma took on difficulties as if fun. This was a child who had a great deal of perseverance. She would do lessons repeatedly to master them and once mastered she'd move on to something that was more difficult. She also became a leader with the other children and they all adored her. Sometimes, Emma could be bossy with the other children, but even so they continued to look up to her with admiration. I knew that this was a child who was a born leader because everything seemed to come easily to her and if this was not the case, she continued to work at it with that huge heart of hers.

When we were children my younger brother had a hard time learning how to read. He struggled and more than likely had undiagnosed dyslexia. In turn, he was labeled which began his struggles with school. This challenge was topped off for him with older siblings who never experienced difficulties with learning especially with reading. My brother was far from dumb and when his IQ was tested my parents were surprised to learn that he was at a genus level though one would never have guessed this by his grades in school. The struggles continued until he made his way to junior college. At that point, he met other people who he had some things in common with. He realized that he had a gift for being able to take electrical things apart and to then put them back together. He also found that he had an ability to do higher math which no one else in the family could in any way or form come close to tackling.

My brother went onto the University level and became a mathematical engineer. This child who once struggled academically is now a very successful adult. He is an example of a person who had to find his own particular niche because he was a "different learner."

Contrarily, while I excelled with reading and writing I was lost early on when it came to math. Math, consequentially is a subject that is learned in a step by step process so when one step is not understood progression often doesn't happen. In my case, my teachers even straight out said that I was a lost cause. I dropped out of my algebra courses and gave up on the idea of learning higher math with the belief that it was "beyond" my abilities. However, as an adult teaching in a Montessori school I was able to view different ways in which math was taught including the use of counting beads, blocks and other tools which made the process fun, entertaining and even attractive. I knew then intuitively that it wasn't my lack of ability that held me back with math, but was the fault of the *way* that this subject had been taught to me.

As a teacher, *my* greatest gift has always been my ability to love the children who had the most difficulties--at least *most* of the time. I found these children compelling, intriguing and certainly in need of understanding. I *wanted* to reach out. I wanted to make a *difference* in their lives.

It's not always easy these days to touch upon that *need* or to find a way to teach *differently*. Schools restrict, mandate and pressure certain regulations even within preschools. Children are expected to sit at circle times and follow rules. The reality is also that we *need* rules or classrooms would be chaotic, but not every child falls into specifics.

The spiritual adult needs to find ways that touch upon the core of the child. When we can achieve this goal we help the child to feel a confidence with their academic and school life. When we are able to give a child a sense of triumph when learning we offer a great gift that benefits the child. The child then can see a purpose for learning within him or herself and this promotes confidence even with challenging situations.

While studying education I learned about <u>Multiple Intelligences.</u> This is a theory developed by Howard Gardner who suggested that there are **seven** different styles of learning. I think that in a world where children are labelled with various learning disabilities, autism, ADHD and so on it is encouraging to learn of various methods to teach individuals. The seven styles of learning according to Gardner are:

<u>Linguistic Intelligence</u> which involves sensitivity to spoken and written language. These kinds of learners are often our poets, writers, lawyers and speakers.

<u>Logical-mathematical intelligence:</u> this learner is easily able to analyze problems logically, carry out mathematical operations and investigate issues scientifically.

<u>Musical intelligence</u> involves performance, composition and the appreciation of musical patterns. Gardner says that this form of intelligence runs in an almost structural parallel to linguistic intelligence.

<u>Bodily-kinesthetic intelligence</u> is where the learner acquires understanding best when able to use his/her body parts to solve problems. This relates to both mental and physical activity.

<u>Spatial intelligence</u> is when the learner can recognize wide and confined space and use this for learning.

<u>Interpersonal intelligence</u> is when the learner achieves the most through the usage of his/her feelings and emotions

appreciating fears and motivations for learning and progressing.

Gardner further claims that most people have a **blend** of these learning styles.

Now, if we were to seriously contemplate the validity of these seven learning styles, we may have to reroute our entire way of teaching to formulate methods that work for individual children within a group structure. Many parents have seen benefits of homeschooling so that their individual child's needs are met, however, the social needs of the child may be lacking in *this* setting. The quandary of achieving the most for the individual learner continues and is a non-ending aspiration for those of us who care about the child.

What do you think? How do you think that children learn best? How do you yourself learn?

I also hold that nutrition plays a huge role in how children and adults absorb information. For instance, children mature earlier when raised on foods that include animal hormones and antibiotics and this is not a positive thing. For instance, in one class that I taught a four year old little girl was already developing breasts! As a vegetarian, I believe that animals have their own karma and when we eat animal products our bodies also then absorb that karma which we then need to process. Internally, this creates challenges for everything in our lives. Carbs like pasta are hard to digest and are heavy in the system. Increasingly people presently are becoming aware of how gluten effects the body and causes all kinds of ailments. On the other hand, when children are raised on food that is a source of the light they are often more active, energetic, balanced and able to retain information. Food that comes from light sources are those that grow from the ground; these are primarily vegetables and fruits.

Detachment

Sensitive people often take on the lives of their children, parents, friends and coworkers. We bring them home with us in our pockets, think about them and imagine what they are doing during time away from them. We love them and want the best for them. However, there will be confrontations, challenges and disagreements that will take you to the edge. It can be hard.

Someone once told me that the world as we see it is composed of our reactions and if you want for your life to change, change the lenses of your glasses. To simply change the way that you look at what happens in your life sounds like a great recipe for a good life and seems simple, doesn't it? Yet, it's hard to change. Often we get caught within what we feel at any given moment and unfortunately this is what the Universe picks up from us and is then manifested into and as our lives. For this reason, our lives are our own creations because our thoughts, reactions and actions are our realities.

Once when reactive where I worked I often felt frustrated, annoyed and disgruntled. Yet, somehow, grace came into this picture and I started to see how I had created this situation for myself. I saw how I was more involved in the conflicts than I had anticipated or would have liked to admit to. When I was able to witness how my reactions had caused a way of life which made me unhappy I disengaged and became detached. Sounds cold, huh?

Then, I told my coworkers that I was detaching myself from them and they too thought that this sounded cold. My new stance didn't sound kind to them, but after a while they saw a different me. I was calmer. I was smiling and even often laughing. I was joyous and able to give love. This new state that appeared so easy going and harmonious came from becoming detached because when I no longer reacted to whatever was going on outside of myself I was at peace. Further, when peaceful I was able to see more clearly. I could see the whole picture and not just an aspect that caused frustration. I learned that when in a state of detachment rather reaction I am able to see what is truly happening for others and for me. I then took things less personally and was able to move on with my life with more direction.

It took effort to get to this point of clarity for me. I had to work on not reacting. I learned to take breaths before speaking, to pause and to contemplate what was coming up for me. I found that the practice of detachment is not one of shoving life under a carpet and singing, "Que Sera Sera, whatever's meant to be will be!" No, this is not what I want because this would be to give up control of one's own life. I learned that you have the power to create your life, but that this takes work. This exertion involves examining your emotions as they come up on a deep level. When you contemplate your emotions as they come up layers and layers of old patterns are revealed for you to then change.

For example, you might have a coworker who annoys you because she says things that ignite your competitive spirit in a way that isn't always kind. You blame her. You say things that may even pull her down--just a tad and you laugh at her behind her back. Meanwhile, the relationship between the two of you gets increasingly unbearable. Your boss even calls you into her office because of the squabbling. You sit there and you feel ashamed, embarrassed and even in denial. You didn't do anything after all because she started it! Sigh... If only you had contemplated what was causing you to feel the way that you did when you met this coworker. You may not have blamed her and instead you may have even been able to clear out some old patterns of behavior of your own. Think about what could have been if you had been detached rather than reactive. You may have seen an old insecurity of your own that made you feel anxious and therefore competitive and when you witnessed this within yourself you could have had compassion for yourself and even for your coworker. However, even in the worst scenario it's not too late to make a change as I believe that these things come up so that we are forced to look at them.

Life can often become competitive. I found it odd in teaching because it is a field where we so readily give our hearts to the children, but competition happens when people are more in-tune with their egos than they are with their hearts. We forget to simply be *who we are*. When competition roars its ugly head it can put people at odds with one another and it can make it difficult to form heart connections. This then seeps into everything that we do. It is destructive and it hurts everyone involved including and maybe especially the children who we love. In competition, we have lost our sense of childhood trust for humanity and this devalues who we all are.

I've experienced this repeatedly from both sides. I know what it feels like to be competed with and to feel insecure enough to compete. The reality is that it takes a great deal of internal work to avoid falling into the pitfalls of the ego. Truthfully, we are all mirrors of one another. When you begin to feel threatened by a coworker, relative or friend for whatever reason it is time for you to go inward and find out what is causing this. You need to do the internal work that is necessary so that you can be the great person that you were meant to be.

The first step that is needed is for you to check your feelings. Stop reacting to what comes up and become a witness. Observe your emotionality from a detached point of view. Meditate on this and allow yourself to go into a deep place where the emotion is coming up whether this is your heart, your belly or place of power. Simply notice if there is fear, sadness or anger and let it be for a moment without any judgment. Contemplate what has come up for you through journal writing and when you are done let go of the negativity. Hold onto the fact that you have been brave enough to do this and that you have exercised the negative patterns of emotion out of your system. You are free of what has held you back previously.

In doing this you are giving yourself a great gift because it will literally lighten your load. Consider too that when you are feeling less anxiety, anger, resentment, etc., you are also then able to give to other people what they deserve from a higher perspective. You are able to offer from your heart a wholeness that is from the core of who you are as a spiritual person. It is refreshing to do this because it takes you back to the place of newness from the time when you easily gave of your heart as a child. You become that new and fresh spirit with an experienced adult's point of view and this is the best that you can be because you have both light and the wisdom.

There will always be times when you are stretched and when your buttons are pushed, but when you have tools to help you with these times you can get through them with ease. You learn from these situations and become a better person. For instance, several months ago I felt emotionally attacked due to words said by someone who I cared for. Initially, my reaction was to strike back, but instead I contemplated what came up for me. I took responsibility for my feelings and actions which made it easier for me to let go of the confrontation. I decided then that the relationship was more important to me than was being "right." When I saw that person again it was as if this conflict never occurred and I was not only relieved, but joyous because of the love that I hold for the person which matters more to me than does any competition.

Smile. Difficult people are blessings because when we don't react to what they seem to put out we all evolve. Learn to detach, to contemplate your emotions as they come up and go deeper to see your own patterns of behavior. You will be able to make changes in yourself and then in your life. You will manifest greatness for yourself and for other people in your life because they too will see the light that is you.

Money and Worthy Wages

Some people appear to have it all as if born into it. You know the types...those with "old money" who have never had to work a day in their lives as we struggle to pay the mortgages on our tiny homes.

It can seem a bit unfair, but what if the cosmos were more sophisticated than this? Perhaps there is an "equalizer" besides death. Perhaps we move through lifetimes with lessons to learn and in each we gather information for a higher purpose. Maybe previously money was never an issue, but was taken for granted eliciting the lesson of respect.

At any rate, I think that there are cycles to life which teach and promote betterment.

I wasn't born to a wealthy family, but we were certainly not poor either. We had a lovely home, family and love that we shared in abundance. When I reached adulthood and became a teacher I didn't make much money especially at first. It felt that there was constant worry just to pay the bills and I didn't handle it well. I took out credit cards and when one got too big, I took out another to pay the first off. It was kind of crazy and led to many sleepless nights.

For a long time I held money as "Evil," "Dirty" and that which the "Greedy" held. Money almost felt sacrilegious, but I was **wrong**.

I remember one evening when it all started to change. I decided to pray. I had only recently met my teacher and dressed in a sari to do my former little Catholic girl novena to the Goddess Lakshmi who represents abundance, wealth, love and beauty. It was very ritualistic at first, but something happened on the very last night of this. There kneeling on the floor in front of the alter that I had prepared I had a clear and beautiful vision. I started to cry because I suddenly realized how blessed I was and was filled with gratitude. I knew then that gratitude creates abundance. Abundance absolutely goes hand in hand with gratitude.

My financial situation didn't change for a while, but maybe a year later I was offered an opportunity to spend a summer with my teacher in upstate New York and while there I met another woman whose situation was not unlike my own. She told me her story of change. Hers was like mine in that it felt like nothing moved financially which caused constant struggle. However, she saw how her belief system which included the *need* to struggle created her life and she decided to change her relationship with money. She went back to school and with *enthusiasm* started her own business. She began to see herself as a form of God. She rejoiced in this and suggested that I do the same.

When I listened to her I remembered my novena to Lakshmi and was struck because I realized that this goddess of abundance is inside us all. We are all beautiful, loving and capable and this is a Universe of "what we give is what we receive."

That evening I dressed again in my prettiest silk sari for a program with my teacher who gave what is called, "Darshan" which is where the teacher blesses the students one by one as they line up to give gratitude and receive blessings. When it was my turn I was suddenly told to stop and stand before my teacher who with her beautiful wand of peacock feathers bathed me with her love while going over my body from head to toe for several minutes with the cascading wand of feathers. When she did this she affirmed to me that my realization of inner abundance was correct.

Slowly, my feelings about money changed. I learned to give more and to hold on less tightly and found that this creates flow. I also developed **respect** for my finances. I paid attention to them. I stopped using credit cards and only paid in cash or didn't buy. I was grateful for what I had and learned to be content when I didn't have. I held firmly that there was a flow and began to see money not as "evil" or "dirty" but as a form of God.

Thankfully, I am no longer in debt other than my relatively (as mortgages go) small mortgage and I always feel that the Universe takes care of me. I am also more inclined to donate because I believe that when we give we also receive.

Money comes and goes, but with the allowance of flow, gratitude and respect my money tree always provides what I need and more.

Recently, I've worked toward taking a greater stand for myself which included being in the present moment and believing in my own greatness. When I did this I decided to also take a stance that I had held close to my heart for many years which is the fate of finances for teachers especially those who work in early childhood education.

Several years ago, I accompanied coworkers to Sacramento which is the capital of California. We went there specifically to rally for what was called, "The Worthy-Wage Campaign." It was an exciting time as we journeyed by Amtrak and carried picket signs that we made for this rally. We took a stand for teachers and especially one which was for those working with young children so that they could be paid better.

Most of my friends and coworkers earn more than what is the national rate of pay on average for teachers of young children, and yet, we complain and we have the right to do so! Most of us have beyond Bachelor of Arts degrees, some of us have Masters, most have teacher credentials and many have years of experience still we struggle financially.

Education begins within the first four years of life. It has been stated that these primary years are the most influential of all. Maria Montessori stated that children under go what she called "sensitive periods" where learning can take place. She said that children have periods of life where they are more acutely sensitive to learning and developing. If these times are recognized and utilized, learning is achieved quickly and easily. However, if these periods are not seen, the learning will be forever lost! Teachers are trained to observe the child and are then able to recognize these stages. It takes money to train teachers so that they are able to do this important work. Shouldn't it then take money to keep teachers trained and interested in this career?

The fact is that this field has lost many teachers due to finances. Talented teachers become disheartened by the rate of pay that they have received and leave the field for pastures with more money. Who really loses when educators leave the field? Obviously the children lose potentials. Conversely, however, we all lose because the children are the future and like it or not this future effects us all--young and old...

The stand that I take is for teachers of young children to be given the pay that their work deserves. Teachers deserve to be paid a wage that is worthy of the greatness that is this profession!

It is a hard profession that often results in burnout and the low pay does not help. It has, however, taught me about "Frugal living!" As a teacher and I've never made tons of money, however, I'm also not in debt unlike the majority of Americans. How have I done this?

For the most part the answer to the above question is, "I live simply to simply live." Yes, this has been said before, but there is truth to this which is remarkably appealing.

I am happy and live with grace. I do well for myself and have always been independent. Frankly, I hold that what I "need" is always available to me. First, I take stock of what I need before I grocery shop and for the most part (flexibility is good) I stick to a plan. I buy quality clothes that I know will last which may mean waiting for sales. I take *care* of myself so that my health is good and enjoy the things in life that are free. I love to go for long walks for instance. You'd be amazed at how well walking can lift the spirits plus it keeps the body in shape. Walking is fun. I take my camera with me which is something that I enjoy.

Frugal living doesn't mean "penny pinching." Frugal living can be as simple as being conscientious of *how* you spend your money which also includes paying your bills on time so that your credit score stays good. If you do this, you also avoid costly late fees which can be exorbitant. These kinds of unnecessary fees can eat away at your savings and bring down your credit score so pay your bills on time.

If you are having money issues or have lost your job, many companies will work with you. PG&E, for instance, has a program for people with lower incomes that you can sign up for which drastically cuts your bills and makes them incredibly easier to manage. Check this out and it will also cut your stress level way down.

Take care of your money by *honoring* it. Treat it as if it were something beautiful to behold. Carry your money in attractive containers whether that be a wallet or purse. Someone once told me to never place your purse on the floor because that is to disrespect it. I've found that money comes most readily when we also offer gratitude for it. It's rather amazing because when we are thankful for what we have we often are given more. Furthermore, when we are generous with what we have with other people we also are given more. This is a rule of give and take and ebb and flow that goes with the Universe. Give thanks and be generous and you will never do without.

I've learned, however, that when we live with *desire* we live *without* contentment. When we live in a state where we constantly *want* we are never fulfilled. You know the old story about the man who wanted the bigger house? This man bought house after house and each one was larger than the last as if to make a statement about who he was as a person (Important), but did this man become happier and happier with each larger lot? No, he never reached a state of exult because he constantly strove for more which only created anxiety. When we live with desire we are never satisfied and this elicits fear because what we have becomes never enough. If you recognize your own way of living in this scenario, maybe it's time to make some *internal* changes.

First, if you are in debt, write down everything from your smallest debt to your largest and *examine* this. This process may be painful because most people carry shame about debt, but if you avoid it and don't confront it, the issues continue. Your spending habits that have gotten you into debt will not change because this way of life is extraneous as it seeks external rewards ultimately leaving you dry. Take the time and have the courage to look at *why* you have gotten yourself into debt.

There was a time in my life when I had serious debt with student loans to high priced purses. I was miserable and had to make big changes in how I addressed my spending habits. This ultimately elicited a need to look at *why* I had acquired these habits which brings us back to the subject of "need." Do you really *need* yet another pair of Gucci shoes? Probably not... What I learned when I did this self-inquiry is that I was okay with two pairs of nice shoes instead of thirty pairs of crappy ones. I was also able to take the time to save the money needed to buy quality shoes which made them more special than they would have been if I had pulled out a credit card to buy them on a whim. I *cared* for *how* I was able to buy them which ultimately made me feel better about the purchase made.

You've got to get *real* with *you* or your money issues will never fall in line. You will find, however, that you don't have live like a "Frugal penny pincher" to have great things, to save money and to stay out of debt.

In the end, simply get real with you and with your "needs" and your money will **flow**.

Letting Go of Fear

Several years ago I had the "aha" moment that showed me how powerful fear is and of how people's fear is manifested in a variety of different ways. For instance, I used mine as a shield to protect me by *hiding* from the world. "Hiding" for me created a space where I rarely expressed my feelings, didn't explore, agreed with *whateva*, over ate and more. There were times that I had clarity on what I was doing, but rarely on the reasons for *why* I was compelled to do what I did. Uncovering prompts took self examination which involved deep contemplation of layers and layers that were peeled away. It wasn't pretty and was far from easy, but worth it because years later I feel more content not to mention healthier.

This "aha" moment gave way to insights to other people's manifestations of fear as well. For instance, I saw how some people respond with temper. They explode largely causing others to fear them, but the reason they do this is because of their *own* fear. It's like the scared bully who berates the younger and weaker child. Fear is the *underlining* emotion for other emotions and this gives way to reactions.

Once I worked as a Director for a woman who was starting a new school. This appeared wonderful at first because it was close to home, offered more money than I had previously been paid, and in my estimation, was an opportunity which would become a great learning experience career-wise. I didn't realize then that the kind of lesson that I was about to be given had nothing to do with my career though would change my approach to fear drastically.

Red flags should have waved high and with velocity when I interviewed for this position. The owner took me to dinner and said, "I have a temper. I often yell at people, but don't take this personally, okay? I do it when nervous..." I'm sensitive and I've never been one to appreciate being yelled at, but nodded and said, "No problem!"

On my first day I got to work early and stood in front of the school until the owner's mother who was the school's cook arrived. She was a sweet, soft spoken older woman who welcomed me with huge smiles. I felt a heart connection immediately with her, but when her daughter arrived at the school it seemed that all hell broke loose. She was annoyed with the way that her mother had made breakfast for the children and began to scream. She let it loose with a lack of censorship loud enough for the children to look to me with fear in their eyes. Later that day, the owner continued to hustle children into a van to drive some of them home and as she did this she yelled at each one to hurry up, pay attention and to listen to her. She then turned to me and said in a soft voice, "See you tomorrow!"

I knew by the end of that first day that I had made a huge mistake in accepting this job, but I also had a mortgage and no other job to go to so had to hang in there at least for a while. I tried to make the best of the situation with a cheerful attitude, but the screaming continued which was mostly directed at the school owner's mother and sadly enough toward the children. For a while, I appeared not to be a direct target but, this did not mean that I valued or condoned the nasty outbursts.

Time went by and the school owner's habit of calling the school first thing in the morning to yell at me about something trivial was established. I tolerated this until she began to make these calls after work to my home. I disliked this woman and when she further asked me to sign in absent children's names for her food program so that she'd receive funding illegally I refused and called Child Care Licensing. I knew that this would put my job at risk, but didn't care because I felt strongly that she shouldn't have been in the business of working with children with a tendency for an eruptive temper. Inwardly, I also felt that old familiar fear rise up within me like a dreaded icy rain storm that made my stance of courage hard to keep up.

It was a difficult time because I needed the job financially, but hated it to the degree that I felt afraid to go there due to the stress that the constant confrontations caused me. Regardless, I knew that I wouldn't have been there if I didn't need to learn something from this experience so began to pray for understanding. I prayed and then meditated with hope that I would be guided. I believe firmly that when we I ask for help it does come to us. We simply have to be open and to trust that there is a reason for everything.

With this inward process I began to contemplate what I was experiencing and this helped me to realize that even though this woman appeared exceptionally angry her histrionics were prompted by fear. I saw then that her fear unlike mine which caused me to want to hide was manifested with temper. This showed me that different people respond to fears with a myriad of emotions and that fear is ultimately the basis for all negative emotionality which holds us back from our highest Selves. With this recognition, I was able to hold a realm of compassion for this woman despite that I had previously intensely disliked her. Ironically, I found another job soon after I came to that place of compassion. The lesson that I needed had unfolded to completion and I was then able to move on.

This experience has remained with me because it taught me about how fear is manifested through a variety of emotions. I recognized how I tend to hide when afraid though other people may handle their anxiety in a different and even complete opposite way than how I would. This gave me a new understanding for other people which elicited in me a greater sense of compassion.

The process of examination and awareness helped me to also deal concretely with my own patterns of fear. I saw then how helpful it is to pause before reacting. This enables freedom from the reactions which previously controlled me and therefore guided my destiny.

Some few years ago I taught in a Montessori School after an extensive teaching career in traditional settings. I was hired as a "Head Teacher" which meant that I oversaw a classroom. However, the classroom filled quickly and I needed help. The owner then hired a woman who had more Montessori training than I did. The owner stated clearly that we would "team teach" and that although this other teacher had more Montessori training than I did this in no way would undermine my education and experience. It was all good until we started to work together and the differences in style became blazingly apparent which elicited insecurities for both teachers as we questioned each other constantly as to "why are you doing it *that* way...?" I wanted the class environment run one way, she wanted it another, and there was simply no middle ground for either of us. I was miserable and I suspect so was she.

The following year that teacher moved on to another classroom and an "aide" entered the classroom to work with me. This time, the aide had **no** education, but happened to be one of the school owner's childhood friends. She was insecure about her position, lack of education, etc., and this was expressed with blaming as well as a great deal of absenteeism. If anything went wrong, according to her, it was my fault and she detailed this to the extreme to her friend, the school's owner. I bit my tongue a lot during that year, but it was hard because my feelings were often hurt and I felt anxious about my job.

By the end of that year, however, I began to examine my feelings of anxiety, frustration, anger and discontent. I realized where I had gone wrong with the first teacher who had been assigned to "Team teach" with me. I felt ashamed of how I had responded to her and talked with her about this. I told her of how I had felt threatened by her and explained that my feelings had nothing in reality to do with her personally and everything to do with how I viewed myself. I confided in her that my insecurities had hindered my ability to allow for individual freedom of expression for both of us. When I opened up she then also admitted that she had similar feelings which impeded upon her ability to team teach due to her own vulnerabilities. This conversation paved a way toward understanding and to becoming friends. Through this opening of the heart I was able to see the value that she had as an educator as well as a fellow human being. Furthermore, I knew that if she and I were to team teach again, we would have an entirely different experience than we did previously because both of us had reached a place of honesty with our self-doubts. We took responsibility for how we had handled the situation and came to terms with better possibilities for ourselves as teachers and as authentic people.

This term authenticity, however, has varied implications for different people. Still, authenticity connotes being real with other people; getting down to the core of the truth and taking responsibility for one's actions like my former coworker and I did. It's not always easy to do, and yet, it is appealing because when a person has become truly authentic that person becomes trustworthy. When we are authentic with ourselves we trust our own decisions. This does not mean that our lives suddenly become one hundred percent rosy because it involves challenge. Getting real with ourselves is hard. Getting real involves digging deep within to the surface of our issues to make changes within ourselves, however, when we do this the rule of truth and honesty truly become golden.

Less authentic people do whatever that they feel is necessary to get ahead regardless of their internal rules. This can mean lies told about another person to create a position for themselves; backstabbing someone who has been a friend or even an advocate. Internal rules go by the wayside, but the question then becomes about the quality of life.

Remember that old adage of looking at the person in the mirror and "seeing" that person? When a person has come to terms with their authentic self there is nothing in that mirror that elicits shame. The authentic person is not mistake free. Everyone makes blunders, but that authentic person takes responsibility for the mistakes made and learns from them.

The challenges that I have mentioned here gave me the "aha" insight that I could be me with my own particular authentic style of teaching and for living my life, that I could also give space to another person whose style may be unlike my own and work together freely while valuing the differences that we have to share. I learned that dissimilarities don't have to create "right" or "wrong." I also learned from working with the aide that I don't have to take on a blame and shame game that is based on someone else's insecurities. I learned not to take personally the back bites from another person who is insecure because truly this behavior has nothing to do with you and everything to with the person casting the stones.

I found then that a more holistic approach to life elicits humor. With this way of living we can see the silliness that is within all of us humans and find compassion because we see ourselves in other people. With empathy we can laugh and share in our journey toward betterment together knowing that we all have work to do, and in the end, this work creates bonds. It is challenging, but with laughter there is also light and with light there is joy regardless of tribulations. This expedition creates a union that provides a sincere effort toward becoming real with ourselves and this takes us deeper into the heart of the human.

In that deep place of the heart we are open to learning and this allows for a synchronicity that constantly reveals "aha" moments to take place over and over. This elicits understanding of the Self for a more positive approach as well as offers compassion for other people. When we have reached this state we are able to give to our children, friends, family and coworkers from the heart because we have become elevated to a place of love instead of one that is based on competition and fear. This is freeing so that we can be the best that is possible for us to be. When we become free of fear we are clear of our callings and we are also able to see this in other people despite dissimilarities.

Becoming free of fear allows for us to be authentic as human beings.

However, sometimes people lose perspective. In this cycle of abuse that fear has caused we develop an insistence on being "right" regardless of what that means or how we come about getting that big "Win." We belittle and berate others as well as ourselves with disregard when we promote ourselves as "Better than." Yet, is this self congratulation in any way a real possibility and or even ultimately important?

It is easy to fall into this pattern of exploitation at times. We use self grandiose as a way to create something within our minds that is pure delusion. This inaccurate concept holds no knowledge of who we are fundamentally as our most true selves. As we go through our lives holding onto this untruth we unfortunately lose the sense of hope that was once engraved as part of the Self within. We lose that touch of humanity for others as well as for ourselves when we do this.

This division creates boundaries which not only separates us from our own hearts, but also forms barriers that make it impossible to connect on a soul level with other people. When we do this we make sure that the other person walks away knowing that we have succeeded in making them feel somehow "Less than." However, do we feel better about ourselves after we have created a shallow box for another human being, and in the end isn't it our own perceptions that we have really judged?

Arrogant adulation for petty vilification is nothing but a hinderance to liberation and to freedom from suffering.

Some people may hold that life is meant for suffering and that this is the purpose of life's essence, however, I believe instead that we are meant to go beyond the point of suffering and to even end it. This, I also hold cannot happen without deep penetration into the psyche of the mind that is beyond the ego.

There was a time in my life when I valued the darker times. I wrote sad poems and labored in this state. Tribulations of course make us grow. Challenges make us stronger. Yet, as I now succumb to the journey of life as a process of hope I become expanded into the human divine which holds the light. As this happens, I cannot relinquish my desire for human expectation of reverence for the divine over petty entitlement and hold tightly onto what I believe is the highest for that will take me to the place within that is the absolute. This intention elicits my fundamental persuasion to conquer the small which if I were to hold onto, would deliver me only to the fatality of my expansion.

I hold that we are all One. We are one spirit, one heart and one mind within the form of many!

Contrarily, when we see ourselves as separate from others we use belittling remarks that rip at other's hearts. These attempts at self promotion penetrate deep within our own hearts and bring us to a place of disengagement which creates a hollow sense of power. How can we defend the ability to persecute the very Self that is within all? How do we continue to impair the sense of Universal attentiveness to the soul when we are biting at another for self gain and what are we acquiring when we sacrifice our integrity? Ultimately, this only creates a loss for both parties.

We lose our hope for freedom when we dispose of human compassion.

Can we instead rise above our petty inclusive need for self importance and value the greatness that is within all of us equally? If we can achieve this even for a moment greater times of true freedom can arise within us for a life that gives human hope.

Let us all make the intention of freedom a goal.

Acceptances of Differences: Cultures

Years ago I argued with someone who I valued in my life and this left me in tears. However, what was elicited then was something said to me by my older brother which was, "The people who we love the most are not always what we 'want' them to be." I had a lesson in tolerance; in acceptance, forgiveness and in compassion.

The majority of people have expectations for others based on standards that they use for themselves and this can be eye opening even for the most spiritually oriented. Most people don't question the reality of these guidelines for other people because what has worked for them is expected to be adhered to by another unquestionably. And why not? After all, this comes from a matter of ethics even when 'personally' based.

Most people don't question the ethics that they hold almost as rights to breath, although, these principles were taught to them. People learn ethics from their parents, families, close friends, teachers and other society members. People are influenced by churches and the government. What is taught becomes inclusive creating expectations that others act and believe in a particular way that is similar to what is known.

Still, America is thought to be a melting pot of cultures. Most American people are products of immigrants from first or several generations ago, and yet, in today's climate there is an abundance of bigotry toward those not born in America especially when accents are difficult to understand.

In essence, there is a great deal of anger presently because jobs are outsourced or given to immigrants who don't speak English well though will take a much lower wage than the average American will accept. Some of the bitterness may be warranted because it's frustrating to apply for job after job just to learn later that said jobs were given to immigrants. However, the reality is that once upon a time our forebears were also immigrants who struggled to find work and with luck, ingenuity and perseverance they managed to carve out lives here for themselves and for their future generations. With that in mind, can the average American who is struggling today take out his or her frustrations on the immigrant? In all fairness to the history of the great country called America such intolerance is not ethically based.

Yet, in today's climate of frustration it is easier to take out the boxing gloves on someone other than the person in the mirror, however, perhaps tolerance and acceptance are needed for both parties including the one in the mirror. Perhaps that person staring back at you with your own eyes needs compassion also.

Sometimes, it is best to take a deep breath and allow the time of the circumstances to simply unfold. This, however, can be easier said than done in times of stress, but when we count the blessings that we have in our lives including the blood of those perseverant ancestors we know that we can get through challenges. We know also that we can extend a gracious hand to other people who may be dissimilar to ourselves.

Ultimately, when we embrace cultural differences as well as those of opinions and ethics that are dissimilar from our own we come to see union at work. We come to see that there are common grounds such as the need for acceptance because truly when we hold other human beings as we would ourselves despite disparities seen we come to recognize deep parts of ourselves that are often not acknowledged. We come to value the human race and we come to know our own dignified and great hearts that embrace differences with acceptance and even a little word called love.

The reality is that everybody has different perceptions of ethics, however, too often people tend to validate their own peculiar set of ethics depending on how these serve themselves.

Is it selfish to help oneself? Of course not, but let us look at ways that we help ourselves and determine if we are also helping others or if we are hurting our fellow human beings in the process.

When we take a certain position in life whether that be a leadership role or a friendship we accept a degree of responsibility. We then can't ignore and say, "It's not my business" to ask questions, explore avenues and to care because it *is* your business. It is your business to follow through with what you have started in good consciousness.

Still, it is acceptable in life to change our minds, right? Life would become stagnant if we didn't make changes. Thus, we can both go with the flow and we can make alterations when we feel that this is needed. Does this mean, however, that we get to stop midstream and pull out without giving reasons to our friends, employers, employees, coworkers, etc.? I don't think so and tend to believe that if we do this, we will have to go back in time either in this lifetime or in another to reroute what we started. This is true because when we start something however small or large we have created karma. Karma is simply an action that has a consequence and all actions have consequences.

My perception of ethics in leaving a role is that we need to do it right so not to create more karma and hopefully to dissolve the karma that we have already produced. We need to be clear with both ourselves and with other people. Proper closure in all situations removes the potential for future karma. Be fair, kind and truthful.

Sometimes things get tricky, however, especially when it involves the mighty dollar bill. When this happens friendships can go out the window and loyalties seem to no longer matter. Again, I don't think that you owe your life to another person including an employer, but do it right because what goes around **does** come around. This can be challenging. I was asked by an employer who wanted to hire me if I intended to stay at her place of employment for a long time. I wanted to say yes and to give a "commitment," but the reality is that when karma ends so does the relationship and often we don't have full recognition of what our karma is with a person or place initially. I have found that since I've been on a fiery spiritual path my karma tends to burn quickly thus I don't tend to stay in any one place for a very long time. I do, however, try hard to create closures that are positive so not to create new karma.

In the business world and even sometimes in social situations too often women's voices are not taken as seriously as are men's. This seems especially true if the man is older. He can even be a cranky old man, yet, his tone of contention is seen as "knowledgable" while a woman's information is brushed aside even when what she has said is as valid as is what he had to say. Unfortunately, this seems to be even more common with how women treat other women as women tend to value men's opinions more than they do other women's.

Regardless, most of us want friendships that are empathetic and sensitive women tend to give this in spades, but do we stand by our female friends? Often times if this involves money, women leave their female friends hanging to dry just to impress a man. Will this man care if these women who have followed his advice land flat on their butts? Probably not, however, their former female friends will perseverate on what went wrong and may even offer to help despite the lack of loyalty that was shown to them.

Ethics. How do you treat other people? Are you fair in your relationships? Are you upfront in your dealings with other human beings? Are you honest? Will you stand by your friends?

Think about this because how you treat other people is observed by our children and can promote unethical behaviors into future generations. The children are little sponges that watch and learn from you whether you are giving a "lesson" or not. They admire and look up to you and they see how you treat other people. They observe how you handle conflicts, challenges and disagreements. They know intuitively when you are hurting and when you are frustrated even if you are smiling.

Ultimately, if we are not treating those around us fairly and with ethics, the children observe this. They, in turn, learn through us how to treat other people and this culminates into methods that may not be kind, pleasant or ethical. They have learned through our interactions that cheating is acceptable, betraying friends is part of getting along and that sneakiness is tolerable.

We are surprised when we observe children in sports push their best friends out of the way to make a point or sneak a glance at their neighbor's test, but should we really be shocked by this when we have not taken a good look at what we've taught them through our own interactions with one another? Have we taught them to honor their friends? Have we instilled in them that differences regarding cultures, ways of acting and thinking are interesting or something to be wary of?

It is important for us as spiritual people to be accountable for the world at large because this is the planet that the children will inherit from us. We have the duty to see to it that the children know how to care for the planet and for its entire nation of people regardless of cultural differences. To do this we must take the initiative to show them with our actions that all people matter and that alliances created with honesty are important. This is a basic lesson that starts with us and trickles down to the children. It is a teaching tool that will stay with them for the rest of their lives and that will affect how they will deal with other people as they mature.

As spiritual people we recognize that the children are the basis for how we go about the actions that we take in our lives. With this acknowledgment we take the responsibility of caring for humanity. This care permeates into the Universe and creates better possibilities for relationships that honor one another. This becomes a great offering of love that we are privileged to bestow onto the children. When we come from a place of sincere honesty the children observe our inward integrity.

However, the most ethical person's honor can be unfairly judged and it can be hard when your integrity as a spiritual person is questioned. Has this happened to you? How did this make you feel?

Once, years ago after hiring me my boss said, "I hired you because you have *integrity.*" I was twenty-seven and unsure sure of what she meant by "integrity." I was honest, did what I felt in my heart and this came naturally to me so her comment baffled me. Why would this be an issue for *anyone?*

A couple of years later when I saw deception and manipulation by this same boss I wondered if she remembered why she chose me or at least if she recalled the particular word that she used when she hired me. Did she forget her *own* integrity or was this a word that she simply threw around?

Perhaps in work situations it's easy to disregard one's integrity in pursuit of the dollar bill. We ignore our conscious and blame it on the job as something that we 'had' to do, right? After all, we live in an *"anything* to get ahead" world, but when we are older what do we tell our grandchildren about how we lived our lives?

Work aside, do we live with integrity in our *personal* relationships? What does this mean with the exchange of self in friendships?

I used to think that honesty regardless of heart equated integrity in personal relationships. However, did it really serve my friend to know that I didn't approve of her new boyfriend? I may never know if this helped her or not because that friend never spoke to me again.

Later I asked myself, "Is it important to share your *every* opinion?"

I realized that my ego prompted this sharing. After all, why did I believe that my opinion was more important than were my friend's feelings? I overstepped and gave an opinion that hurt regardless of whether it was "honest" or not.

I learned the hard way when I lost a beloved friend that integrity can be defined with silence. It means to honor someone *else's* feelings over your opinions. I also learned that integrity means to stand up for your friends in a way that gives space, honors and is true to the heart. This integrity is to care enough to simply be there with love.

Once when my spiritual path was criticized my integrity was also questioned. When this happened instead of coming from the heart I became defensive and said unkind things about my friend's religion. I payed the "tit for tat" game and went too far which caused a breach of trust. This experience taught me to allow friends to walk their *own* paths within their *own* time and gave me a sense of detachment when others didn't appreciate *my* path. It gave me integrity's freedom.

Integrity comes from the heart and when we check with our hearts before acting or speaking we rarely go wrong.

As spiritual people let us come from that place of integrity showing ethics in how we deal with each other for this is one of the greatest lessons that we can offer any human being.

Synchronicity

Have you ever noticed how in life things come back to you somehow? Life is circular in motion. The energy of life is always moving, and yet, somehow we are often brought back to our roots, where we started and what we dreamed of.

Have you observed that what has come to fruition in your life has often been what you put your attention on? This may be because you've placed effort into building something; a career, home, relationship, but it could also have manifested simply from your thoughts. *Whatever* you put energy into has a way of become realized.

Sometimes we are given hints whether this is from God, the Universe, a High Spirit or whatever you want to call it. We are told to explore and go deeper.

Once, my cousin sent me a picture of the house that I grew up in when my family lived in upstate New York, however, this house is now much bigger than it was when we lived there. Our cute little two story house with the woods in the backyard is **gorgeous** now as the new owners have added additions. Nothing stays the same because everything in life is transitory though there is a pull from the core of who we are that never changes.

The house is often used as a metaphor for the soul.

Does the soul ever really change? Could it be, however, that in our pursuit of expansion toward consciousness when we become more inclined to know our souls this higher Self then feels greater and larger within us? My thought is that this internal greatness was always there within us as large as life though we only come to recognize this with the pursuit of spiritual practices.

I've spent a great deal of time meditating, contemplating and doing self inquiry and this process has opened me to new possibilities. These new ventures may be placed in the future though seedlings are being watered and nurtured in the present.

Still, there is that tie to the past that paradoxically nudges one forward. I've experienced that there may be times when we feel attached to something or someone, but the karma has concluded and our time then in that circumstance ends. However, when something is unfinished or unresolved we are often brought back to it for closure. We are meant to work it out with that person or in a particular life experience. We gain insight into ourselves in this way to make changes and to become greater. We learn to see our mistakes as lessons for self improvement.

Life is circular.

Have you experienced synchronicity? What have you learned from this about yourself?

The other day I overheard a couple arguing. I drank my coffee and tried not to listen, but their voices carried into my stream of consciousness. Apparently, he had upset her and defended himself with, "I am *only* human!" This didn't carry weight with her and it wouldn't with me either. I wanted to yell back, "Take out the '*only*,' buddy!"

Yeah, yeah...we *all* make mistakes and "to err is human," right?

I make mistakes and that's a sure thing. However, when I have contemplated the mistakes that I have made I come to know that I make them when I don't listen to my intuition. Simply stated, my intuition guides me and when I follow it I am mistake free. The trouble is that I don't *always* follow that keen and wise voice within. Why?

I get bogged down. The world becomes a vast and scary place. In my experience, when I listen to my fear instead of my intuition I make mistakes. My friends and coworkers become vessels thankfully as do family members. They give wonderful advice that is perfect--for *them*. What somebody else tells you may be the most sound and intelligent words, but they may or may not be for you. When they are right they come from the heart and resonant with you. How do you know if they resonate? You have to go inward. You have to do your *own* work.

I have always thought of myself as a fairly intuitive person. I used to even think that this gift was just a little *extraordinary*. What I didn't realize is that *everyone* has this gift, but only a few chose to delve deep enough within themselves for the allowance of this gift to manifest. It's true on both accounts that this is within us all and that we must *allow* ourselves this gift.

We live in a world dictated by concepts and perceptions of success. Everyone has ideas of what this means. For one person, success comes when he puts a down payment on the biggest house on the block or wear diamonds and for another it means to own a horse or to be able to put her children through college, yet, for another it is simply to complete a book. It's all perception, and yet, this carries enough weight that it can make us feel *terrible*. Why is this?

It's that old desire thing cropping up again. You know that thing when you want something so badly and finally have achieved it but it's not enough? You want *more*. You want *something* else. This is a non-ending cycle which we put ourselves through and makes us constantly wrong and consistently "not good enough." What else does this elicit? Remember your old friend, "Worry?"

How do you know and when do you feel that enough is enough? When do you feel satisfied and even *content*? Is it possible at all to feel okay and even *good?* Can this state of happiness *last?*

Life...there's that trump card called change that takes you by storm and hits when you least expect it. There you sit in your little corner of rosiness when suddenly you lose your job and you learn too that your wife is having an affair. You collapse. **Damn!**

How do you ride the waves of tribulation that knock you over again and again?

It's not easy. I've been knocked down more than I care to remember, but know that I have to get back up. What choice do I have? Life keeps going regardless of my stupor.

How do *I* get through it all? First, yeah, I cry. I might even scream and my body might react with a bit of illness, but then I force myself to carry on. I have learned to pray and to have faith that these prayers are heard and I **meditate**. Meditation is not just good for the soul. It's good for the **body**. Meditation calms you, but it does much more. Meditation takes you to that place where you hear your internal voice. Meditation takes you to your divinity.

When you meditate your answers are revealed.

When I meditate regularly I *know* when something is about to happen. I may not know what it is, but I have an awareness.

For months, I *felt* a change coming. I didn't know what it was, but I knew that it was **big**. My intuition told me to be aware and that regardless of what happened I would be okay. I knew that I had to trust and when the change did occur it hit **hard** and it *hurt*, but I was emotionally ready. Worry glanced my way, but I didn't fall apart and I knew that I'd get through it and I **will** always.

We *are* human, but don't preface that with the word, "*Only*." We are not *mere* mortals. We have the potential within all of us for Godliness because we have greatness within us. We have light within us and we can manifest what we want. This does not mean that we don't have to meet with life's challenges. Karma. However, these trials make us stronger. They literally dare us to take them on and summon us for improvements.

When life hits me in the face with bold audacity I go within. I mediate and contemplate what has happened. Perhaps I need to make changes in my life and be open to trust.

Listen to your intuition. Meditate and become great! You are so much more than "only" human and so am I! When we see this greatness within ourselves we also see the potential of vastness that is within the children just the way that they are in all of their perfection. We held this once when we were children and through meditation it is ours again.

Life may feel that it is not perfect, and yet, this in The Guru Gita is said in Sanskrit:

"Om purnamamdah purnamidam
Purnat purnamudacyate
Purnasya purnamaday
Purnamevavasisyate."

Transcribed in English:

"Om. That is perfect. This is perfect. From the perfect springs the perfect. If the perfect is taken from the perfect, the perfect remains."

In essence, everything including our hardships are perfect. *Life* is perfect. I am perfect and you are perfect as everyone in our lives are perfect. How loving and compassionate is that?

This is an incredible blessing because it allows us to consider our so-called imperfections as grace-filled and with wonderment. My emotions and mistakes thus help me to *create* change. This ultimately is forgiveness. It allows me to move beyond the state where I berate myself or hold animosity toward another. It allows me to see the perfection in the challenges, the struggles that the children go through and in my persistent faith.

I was young when I met my spiritual teacher and upon meeting her was skeptical to the point of arrogance. The question that surfaced was, *"Who **are** you?"* However, another question was elicited which was, *"Who am I?"*

As a teacher with young children I am spiritually oriented. I have had dramatic spiritual experiences from the Kundalini. These are amazing at any rate and I hold onto them as if treasures.

Still, spiritual friends told me that this path changed their *physical* lives. They made more money, found love, better jobs, homes, etc., but *my* physical life stubbornly stayed the same. It was frustrating because for instance, instead of receiving wealth my credit cards were stolen. I remember one time when I literally fell to the floor in tears. Yet, somehow, I started to trust the process. I surrendered little by little. I absorbed the messages that came to me through dreams and meditations. I contemplated with self inquiry and changes slowly started to unfold. I began to see how this had *become* that. I started to see the meaning in what I was experiencing and in *life*. I saw that the tiny beam of light revealed to me during meditations was my own Self. I knew that this was also within everyone. It is consciousness and is God. This taught me to hold onto trusting that regardless of whatever difficulty that I had to undergo I would still be okay. This gave me a sense of joy that I had never known.

Life is a miraculous process. I think back to times when I came close to losing my life whether this was in a serious car accident, during surgery, being physically attacked or threatened and in each instance there was a certain light that held me **literally**. This light is an energy force that is within us all. During these times I **saw** this beam of luminance come from my heart and surround me enclosing my entire body with protection.

We all have times when we hurt. Yet, I've learned to give my emotional pain to the fire of yoga. How? I visualize myself holding a beautifully decorated tray which holds my pain and I offer it to that fire to burn it out of me. Sometimes, I need to do this repeatedly to cast the pain from my psyche, but nevertheless it works for me. The pain dissolves and I am able to contemplate my emotions with detachment which allows me to make changes.

Change after all *is* life. Therefore, we can't get stuck in pitfalls. We need to keep moving and looking inward for the heart irrespective of difficulties.

This is the *miracle* of *life*.

Where love rules, there is no will to power, and where power predominates, love is lacking. The one is the shadow of the other.--Carl Jung

The Dance

When I was a child I tried to dig a hole in the dirt to attempt to get to the "other side." I knew that there had to be more than "this." I watched the birds in flight and yearned for "more."

As a child I experienced the *etherial*. I still don't know exactly what this was, but I know that I had touched upon something from that "other" dimension. I think that this is true for many children because they are open to what is there.

Growing up changed some of my perspectives. I didn't stop believing that there was more and that we could actually touch upon this. I stopped *caring*. I dove into my life in the outer world. I went to college, got a job, met people, went to parties and life as I knew it took hold. Still, somehow, occasionally I had a glimpse of that something more, something "out there" that was really within me all along.

I became a "seeker." I went to meditation classes. I gave "psychic readings." I read all the books that I could find on metaphysics. I even went back to the Catholic Church that I had been raised with. I wanted *more* than what the outer world had offered, but I had no idea of what that was--not yet, but they say that "when a seeker is ripe a teacher appears" and this is what happened to and for me.

When I met my spiritual teacher I had the curiosity of a seeker and the cynicism of the world. I wanted *proof* that she could "change" and even "transform" my life. It was as if I dared her to take me on, and yet, when I looked her in the eyes I literally saw The Universe. I saw lights. I saw twinkles of stars and knew this was just the beginning. I saw what could be and what is. I knew that this was the "more" that I had yearned for as a child and that if I dove into those huge almond shaped eyes, I would find what I had searched for.

I went home after meeting my teacher and listened to her mantra. I sat in a chair listening and my energy **exploded** within my body taking off like a rocket within me. I felt the divine energy swirl upward spinning around within me. I saw everything while it did this from where my little cat sat outside on my deck to the stars in the Universe and finally I felt it cascading to the roof of my head. It felt like my soul was about to leave my body and fly to those beautiful illuminating stars. Heat rose within and the thought that my body would melt away potently pulsated. It scared me and I jumped to my feet with the hope that this "strange" energy would **STOP!** I had no idea what had happened and went back to the spiritual center to ask one of the monks who laughed and said simply, "The Shakti **LIKES** you!"

Infinity is within us.

Have you noticed how a child may suddenly stop and stare at what appears to be thin air? He is completely absorbed within whatever it is that he sees because there is something there even though it appears to be invisible to the adults around him. The child is in touch with his sense of infinity which somehow we as adults have lost consciousness with. This is always there, but our worldly experiences have taught us to forget and ignore while the child still sees clearly.

Some say that particular children are more sensitive than are others and these children are deemed, "Indigo Children." These children are said to have been born after 1985, however, I know myself that I had visions and dreams as a child that could be considered extraordinary and I was born well before 1985. Many of these "Indigo" children have also been diagnosed with attention-deficit hyperactivity disorder (ADHD). They are said to be empathetic, curious, strong-willed, independent and often considered strange because they posses a strong inclination toward spiritual matters. Quite frankly, I don't know if there are "Indigo Children," but I appreciate the fact that those who hold this theory nurture the child versus drugging with Ritalin, etc. Children naturally see the unknown because they have not been taught to be afraid of what is there. They are open. We, as adults, however, are sometimes frustrated because we don't know what the child is experiencing and that child may therefore challenge us. They don't want to follow rules, they lack patience with standing in lines and are difficult to discipline They also may be aggressive.

It is our choice to attempt to view these particular children as "Difficult" or see them as nonconformist who will eventually be leaders. If we take on the latter perspective, we can nurture their potentials, creativity and listen to their intuition. We cannot hone them into the particular way of being which is typically viewed by society as "acceptable." However, with an open heart we can guide them to an avenue where they can be expressive in a way that is successful in our world though maybe unlike what is the mainstream. One of the best ways to do this is to meditate with the children. Teach them while they are young to work with their internal divine energetic field and to embrace it. This is part of who we all are though most adults have relinquished this due to fears. Let us instead help our children to embrace this potent part of themselves.

I've found that art is also a very effective tool to help children to become more centered within themselves. Exploring art is fun and it offers a way for the child to go inward without feeling pressured to perform. It always amazes me when I see children create with art materials when they are presented in a simple way without explanation or preconceptions. This offering of adventure allows for exploration of the child's senses. For example, I have often taken nature walks with children to gather anything that we have found interesting. I make no judgments about what we find and then have placed these items on trays with glue, paint and other materials to allow the children freedom of expression. Some children use scant materials to say a great deal while others use every bit of whatever they've found to describe their inner worlds with their own particular formation of art.

As adults it is very important for us to listen to children. The children have much more wisdom than we as adults give them credit for. I've seen teachers and other adults attempt to persuade children to try various things that they may not want to do for various reasons whether this was with foods, going down a slide or a myriad of things. Naturally, we want for the children not to be afraid and to try things, but at the same time we need to extend respect for their feelings and for their intuition which is their internal guide. A few years ago, I taught a little boy who was so afraid of the garbage truck that when it drove near the schoolyard his arms literally trembled. At first, we attempted everything that we could to help him to feel secure. Still, we held great concerns because this fear hindered this child's play during outside time to the degree that this once adventurous child resisted going outside at all. My coworker took him physically to the garbage truck with hopes that this would calm his fears to no avail. My intuition told me that we would not be able to understand what triggered what we judged as an extreme reaction. His fears more than likely stemmed from a past life experience which we had no way of knowing or understanding. I knew, however, that we needed to accept the situation for what it was. When I had this realization I simply asked that the garbage bins be moved to another part of the yard so that this child didn't see the truck. In doing this it became clear to me that we needed to respect where the child was in that given moment and to honor his feelings.

Feelings after all are energetic. They move, create and they change.

It is said that there are seven major chakras which is a Sanskrit word for the wheels within that spin our energy centers. You can experience this for yourself. Try it. Close your eyes and concentrate on your belly. You will feel the essence of the digestive fire. You might feel heat and emotions like jealousy, anger, lust and so on might develop. Close your eyes again and this time concentrate on the heart. You might shiver for a minute which is common when this chakra opens and then feelings of lightness, joy and even love may come up. The divine energy which is that of the soul and is known in the East as the great Kundalini purifies the chakras. This allows us to go beyond our physical lives within the outer world to see the Universe in all it's glory as we tap into it inside of us while we meditate. Don't be fooled, however, to think that this happens *only* during meditation because this energy never sleeps. It is your intuition. It is that little voice within you that tells you when you meet someone that this is a "nice" person or that this job is "right" for you. However, when you meditate it is then that you experience the splendor of the chakras. The Kundalini is an "intelligent" energy that runs through you as you as your divinity.

When you look up into the sky on a clear night and see a thousand, million, billion **beautiful** twinkling stars aren't you **curious** to know where they are with *yourself?* Don't you ever wonder about the magnificence that is in those lights above you *seemingly* so far away?

Sit in a chair with your feet firmly planted on the floor, close your eyes and listen to the sounds of your breath. Go inward and find that breath in the hollows of your chest. Go there and let this be. You will find that there are infinite possibilities. You will know that you are more than your physical body. You will also know that this is true of everyone and that we are all connected. You will see a light that is more **luminous** than you could ever imagine and someday you may even travel into that light of the Universe for this is your birth right.

We are One with each other and with the Universe. Meditate and begin to know who you are.

When I was in my early twenties I fell in love with the picture of the girl who stood on a cliff and stared at the clouds by Maxfield Parrish called, <u>Ecstasy </u>and I lived with a dancer. My intention for my life was "freedom"--nothing more and nothing less. I wanted what this picture elicited for myself and I still want this for our children. I want this for you too!

It's been several years since that picture elicited my longing, but that drive within me for the thirst of the dance of life is still poignantly reverberant within me. My life is best when like a dance with the spirit within. I sometimes fall or dance too fast for my feet to keep up or just boringly slow, yet, this dance is to the tune of **my** heart beat.

I tend to be stubborn and I don't like to be told what to do, but I'm as faithful as a dog when I believe in something or someone. I will put all my trust and heart into you when you make me want to dance because this elicits the feeling that anything could happen. Drop me or step on my toes and I may never want to dance with you again because if my trust is broken, the relationship of the dance is destroyed. However, when positive and vibrant that dance is fluid. It is the dance of God; the dance of love.

Dancing is meditation in action. It is the energy of the core that is the spirt which has no limitations. When you dance from the heart there are no boundaries. You are unencumbered and can manifest life at its fullest. When you dance or just sway to music often you go into what feels like a trance and in that state you lose awareness of what is around you because you are completely centered in the dance of the heart. It's amazing when that happens!

Have you ever watched children dance? As a teacher I often give children scarves to dance with. I turn on music and let them do whatever they want to. Often this produces what appears to be "circle running." The children follow one another laughing without regard for each other's space, but one time I noticed a particular girl dance. Her arms were spread out as she waved the scarves in the air. Her eyes were closed and her legs moved with grace. Her smile was one of pure joy. I was reminded of the Ecstasy painting because in this child I saw abandonment of all preconceptions, fears, ambitions and worry. She was free to be who she really was and I don't think that this is common at all.

Sitting in meditation is another form of dance because it brings the seeker to that core within which allows for liberation from suffering. It draws emotions forward that are sometimes painful, but creates witnessing for cleansing. When this happens there is room to breath because like a physical dance this is a process that gives way to new opportunities for love of the Self and others.

Life **is** a dance. We have many partners in this dance from the clerk in the grocery store who has learned our first names to our mates. We dance with the children in our lives in the basic way that is strictly from the heart. We move with each person that we interact with in one way or another. This dance can be smooth and graceful or it can step on toes when we forget to allow others their own dance. We break rules, collide, become aggressive, competitive and lose our step. Take a breath and go back inward. Meditate on who you are and *why* you are here.

I've learned that some people truly are here to make money on this planet, to invent things, and to be the doers. They can be bulldozers on their quest. These are newer souls to the world and it is okay for them to do this because this is their dance. While others of us are here to touch upon something within our selves and within others. We are here as healers. This is our dance, but either way in this world we need to find ways to dance together. It's not always easy and sometimes it's best to avoid those whose dance breaks our toes. I've learned too that it's okay to step back from the dance and to let it be.

I still yearn for my Ecstasy as I stand on my own cliff and dance for freedom. This *yearning* is beautiful, fulfilling and exciting.

How about you? Do you like to dance? Do you like to watch the children as they dance?

Take Care of Yourself

Life involves huge challenges for all of us despite whatever career choice that we make. As a teacher I found that these tribulations often came from this particular job's low pay, and lack of respect to the tremendous degree of physical exhaustion that is undergone while working. Still, there are ways that I found that helped with the prevention of "burnout" moreover inspired me enough to want to continue. I think that these ideas can be beneficial for anyone in any career or life adventure.

I became a teacher when in my middle twenties with great contemplation. With a degree in Advertising/Journalism I was a copywriter. I learned quickly that Advertising and Journalism were "cutthroat." I wanted something "gentler." I wanted a career that was *fulfilling*.

My niece was two and despite her temper tantrums (she was **strong-willed**) I loved being around her. I found too that I was nurturing, playful and creative. I went back to school and took courses in education. It's been more than twenty years since then and I don't regret this choice because I think that everything in life happens for reasons, but has it been the career that I thought that it would be? No.

I've often been surprised as a teacher because this profession is just as "Cutthroat" as was advertising. To put it simply, administrators can be undermining, coworkers competitive and parents judgmental. As a teacher you give your heart, work hard and come home with little pay, yet, usually you feel strongly that it's all worth it. You love the children clearly. You take them home in your pockets and **constantly** find ways to improve upon your classroom with newsletters, lesson plans, pictures, projects and more. Still, there are days when you bite your tongue and others when you cry.

I remember one busy day when I was screamed at by a mother because I forgot to give her child cough syrup. I was also yelled at by a coworker when I retrieved a ball that I had bought for my classroom from her yard. I knew too that if I complained, I'd be labeled as "defensive" so learned to become detached emotionally. Detachment is a good skill when teaching! I think that detachment is a good skill for any of life's paths because it teaches you not to take things that happen personally.

The reality is that in any job it can be maddening to try so hard only to feel defeated at the end of the day.

As a teacher, I found that my work with the children was the *"easy"* part. When with them you easily come from the heart and enjoy the children's enthusiasm and spontaneity. This elicits your own and you feel lighthearted. Still, you plan for them and create learning goals for them. You work hard to consider what might help them the most, however, this isn't always what your coworker thinks is the "best" plan. She is competitive and even when she sees a child thriving under your care she seeks to devalue your plans. She does everything that she can think of to destroy the work that you've put into with specific children and complains about your work methods solely to undermine you. Let me tell ya that butting heads with this kind of coworker does no good. I digested that I had to accept situations that I had no control over. I told myself that children learn from different styles and this is true when those styles are embraced, but are they? Too often when there are different styles in the classroom conflicts are elicited which can be ugly and mean-spirited.

The smart teacher ascertains that she has to let go and surrender when teaching because truthfully she has little control of what goes on in the classroom. You can set up the environment to its best advantage which helps tremendously, but ultimately you have to go with the flow. It's a different career than is sitting in front of a computer. You can't push a button for something to work out as planned because the children may resist it due to disinterest, exhaustion, illness, etc., and your coworker may not be supportive.

In my life, teaching has been a great career in many spiritual ways. It's taught me a variety of skills that I would never have learned otherwise. It's not easy though every September I will probably always get excited to see a new group of children and will cry when they graduate in June.

Love, of course, is the chief inspiration that keeps people in the field of teaching. We literally fall in love with the children. We dive into their enthusiasm and are thrilled when we see them make progressions. This naturally helps with the pitfalls, however, there are practical steps that you can take as a teacher to further assist you and I think that these are helpful for anyone in any career. These will keep you healthier, saner and able to ride out the challenges.

As we've discussed in previous chapters meditation is essential for spiritual people. We know by now that it takes us inward to that place where we can ascertain the highest information about ourselves. It is our guiding light literally as we wade through the emotions that come up while living. It also creates good boundaries for us so that we don't take in everything that is energetically thrown at us. We become transparent so that when negativities are hurled our way we are like glass in that these potential insults go through us without sticking to our hearts. It is also grounding which is absolutely needed for spiritual people. Consider your scattered friend. She can't remember where she placed her car keys, is late for appointments and has trouble staying focused on any task at hand. Meditation helps the spiritual person to stay focused, present oriented and cheerful.

Still, there are other practical things that you can do for yourself as well as meditation.

Eat right for one thing. Sounds easy? Nope! Where I used to work almost every few weeks someone brought in cakes, candies and pastries. We celebrated people's birthdays, anniversaries, babies and achievements with treats. Most of these delicious, sloppy goodies were brought in from Safeway. You know those huge messy cakes that have layers upon layer of sugary icings? Yep! You can tell yourself that you don't want to mess up your diet with this stuff, but when it sits directly in front of you or when you watch your coworker gobble it down with a smile on her face you may find that it's not so easy to resist. Beyond the sweet confections of goo there were also the pot luck lunches which consisted of big sandwiches, bowls of pasta and more yummy though fattening delicacies. I most definitely put weight on while working at that job.

I can tell you from personal experience too that having extra weight on a teacher's body frame is physically painful. This is not the profession where we get to sit around so being in good physical shape is imperative. During an eight hour day the average teacher stands for at least six of those hours. She is also running around after the children, playing sports with them and doing a great deal of walking from one area of the classroom and play yard to the other. Teachers need to be able to bend with ease, sit on the floor, and move quickly though gracefully because you have to keep up with the children, yet, be careful because they are small, delicate people who you don't want to trample on. When I had extra weight on my body I often had pain in my hips and back. I didn't sleep well and found myself popping more Advil than I care to remember.

I learned that eating healthfully and consciously is absolutely needed for teaching and for living.

The reality is that very few women and men who I know don't struggle to a degree with food issues whether obese, ten pounds over weight or too thin. This is a common battle and is currently an epidemic with our children. Why has this occurred and what we can do to go about dealing with this? The first step is to look at when this became a struggle for you. My battle with my body started at age fifteen. I was willowy and perfectly content with my body because it could climb, run, dance, jump, etc., and that was all that mattered until the age of fifteen. My mother warned then that my rear end was expanding and my father pointed to football players and said, "Some women look like *them!"* Fear became an understatement and personal body issues along with the weight creeped up. I wanted to hide most of the time and did this with food, baggy clothes and hair that hung in my face and this started a life of dieting.

Wouldn't it have been great if instead of frightening me into dieting my parents said, "Honey, what's going on? How are you *feeling?* Can we help?" We can do this for the children who we love by paying attention to their behaviors and emotions as well as by listening to them. This may not have been done for us as children, but we most definitely can offer this gift to our children and hopefully promote healthier body images than the ones that we were raised with.

From my personal experience I've gone on countless diets that have *always* been successful. I've even been too thin, but mostly just slightly too heavy for my tall though small boned frame. Not only has this been aesthetically unpleasant, but it's also been physically painful with backaches, and more. However, my goal presently is to no longer obsess about food. Have you noticed that the person whose weight doesn't shift is usually not preoccupied with how and what they eat? This person may not be model thin, but is usually healthy and happy and this is why I was drawn to the book, Women Food And God by Geneen Roth.

Like Geneen, I've been a meditator for a long time. I have a deep longing for God and know that this connection is *within*. Still, my spiritual teacher has said that food is often the last of our issues to surrender on a spiritual path. This statement reveals how **powerful** our attachment to food is.

It's common for women to reach for that chocolate cake or bowl of pasta when in emotional turmoil. Sure, it's "stuffing the emotions," but it's also a *disregard* for the emotions. Somewhere in time (age fifteen for me) we decided that our bodies were not good places to be in. The emotions within the body overwhelmed so we left so we left the body to no longer feel the pain. This created a way not only to numb the emotions but to ultimately not even experience them.

While reading this book I acknowledged how odd it is for me as a meditator to realize how often I've left my body in efforts to distract from emotional distress. Has this escape route benefited me? No. The reality is that when we don't deal with our emotions they don't simply go away. They resurface often repeatedly with yet another agenda for turmoil. Geneen suggests that instead of unhealthfully medicating with food we return to our bodies and sense where in the body the pain is whether this is in the belly, heart, etc. When we do this we are able to acknowledge the emotion and witness it without *becoming* this emotion. This process ultimately releases the feelings freeing us of the pain that we once stored within us. If we made this a practice, we'd be in-tune with what our bodies want. We'd also love ourselves with greater compassion *knowing* that we are worthy of care. Geneen says that it's about "kindness." Isn't that both beautiful and profound? I think so.

I've been a vegetarian for over a decade and a half and despite former eating disorders am one of those crazy people interested in nutrition which has elicited different ways of eating.

Once, an Ayurvedic doctor said that my body type is Vata/Pitta and gave me a diet specifically for my body. With this diet I went from a size ten to six and then a size two was often too big. Even though friends said that I looked "skeletal" I was **healthy**. As a teacher regularly exposed to germs it was amazing to never even get the sniffles. However, the diet was restrictive. It was challenging for instance, to go to restaurants because there was rarely anything on the menus that I could eat so this form of living went by the way side. When that happened the weight came back on and I knew that I had to find another way of living that helped me to stay both healthy and slender.

I eliminated all forms of dairy though because I missed yummy yogurts I decided that with osteoporosis in my family dairy is a good thing for me.

My biggest downfall is that I have a **SWEET**, sweet, sweet tooth, but sugar is bad for us, right? Yep, it is. Why? Well, we all know that sugar adds to our thighs and isn't wonderful for the teeth, but did you know that it gets into our cells and alters our metabolism? Sugar leads to high blood pressure, diabetes and more because after eating fructose our bodies produces uric acid which causes an inflammation and an increased ability for cells to become fat. The result is often fatty-liver disease. This disease can lead to liver failure.

We all know that vegetables are our friends, but do you know how to pick those that are the best for you? Dr. Oz says to look for those that have the most brilliant colors-- the more vibrant greens, vivid reds, etc., because these are the most nutritious.

Did you know that flax seed oil not only prevents cancer, but also reduces cancer and can even cure it? According to Dr. Johanna Budwig, the combination of two natural foods cannot only be prevent cancer but can cure it. These are organic flax seed oil and cottage cheese. It has been proven that this combination prevents cancer, arteriosclerosis, strokes, cardiac infarction, stomach ulcers, Prostate, arthritis, eczema and even immune deficiencies.

Dr. Budwig also tells us to avoid hydrogenated, partially hydrogenated and even polyunsaturated oils due to chemical processing that is harmful to the body. She states that these kinds of fats block circulation, damage heart action, inhibit cell renewal and impeded the free flow of the blood and lymph fluids.

Her theory is that the use of oxygen in the organism can be stimulated by protein compounds of sulphuric content which make oils water-soluble and which is present in cheese, nuts, onion and leek vegetables, but especially in cottage cheese. She adds that carbohydrates that contain natural sugar, such as dates, figs, pears, apples and grapes can be included in this diet and that honey is also beneficial as is Vitamin B from buttermilk, yogurt and natural yeast.

The following are some great articles:

http://news.discovery.com/human/sugar-fructose-obesity-diabetes.html

http://www.eatnakednow.com/nakedlifestyle/2011/01/27/eat-to-thrive-fight-the-winter-blues-with-these-immune-boosting-strategies/?awesm=fbshare.me_AZs0l&utm_content=fbshare-js-large&utm_medium=fbshare.me-facebook-post&utm_source=facebook.com

http://health.usnews.com/health-news/family-health/diabetes/articles/2009/04/10/nonalcoholic-fatty-liver-disease-5-tips-for-treatment-prevention

http://www.acutonix.com/episodes/yogurt/

http://www.acutonix.com/episodes/juicing-and-detox/

Eat and be healthy!

As far as exercise I'm not one to love the gym and have had to find ways to get my body moving that I have liked. For me, walking and swimming has helped me to stay in a fairly good physical shape.

Another tool that I incorporated into a daily regime with children when I taught was to do yoga with them. Most children love yoga as long as it's presented in a way that is fun for them. When you do the poses that have animal names for instance they become enthused. While teaching I bought yoga cards with big colorful pictures that I used with the children. When doing this I allowed the children to choose which card that we'd practice with and let the children take turns being the yoga leaders. This was fun and it kept them in shape as well as gave me needed exercise.

Children also love going on walks often. Teachers need to remember to get the parents to sign permission slips which are needed both for Licensing's purposes and for peace of mind. One thing that I did which helped so that these walks could be done with spontaneity was to write these permission forms in a way that allowed for me to take the children out whenever I deemed necessary. Doing this is great when you've noticed much "outside" active energy that needs to be burned off. Still, I made efforts to give the parents as much notice as possible. For instance, I left notes at the end of the day that stated, "We may go for a walk around the neighborhood tomorrow between 9 a.m. and noon." I also left notes on the classroom door. I learned that the more communication that you have with parents about what you are doing in the classroom the better. Most parents will support your attempts for adventure with the children as long as they are aware of your plans.

These walks will help you tremendously. They can take the edge off of otherwise stressful days just because they get you moving and into the fresh air. They also give you new perspectives because you are not stuck in the same environment day after day. I think that taking walks in the middle of the day regardless of what you do as a career will benefit you and assist to improve your work performance because walking gives a restored outlook and new perspective. When I am struggling with a decision, for instance, walking helps me to think more clearly. It brings you closer to your intuition because it moves the energy within you. For this reason, also if I am upset, walking helps me to become calmer.

Pay attention to your body. It will tell you when to slow down, rest and take time for it. When you listen to it this will help you to avoid becoming ill because let's face it working whether in an office or teaching can be hazardous for the health with the amount of germs that we are confronted with on a daily basis. This is a danger that is true for any profession. Try also to drink as much water as possible and to get to bed on time. I laugh at myself when I remember how often I've been tired while working so therefore filled up yet another cup of coffee. The problem, however, with drinking caffeine to get you through the day is that it stays in your system long after the initial high. This residue can wake you up in the middle of the night disrupting your needed rest and will cause tiredness during the next day. This, unfortunately, can become a vicious cycle. The solution that I found for this was water. I bought a canteen type of water bottle that I could refill often and kept it with me during every working day. I sipped and gulped water all day long which kept me from eating the sweets that I otherwise yearned for and gave me needed energy which unlike with caffeine did not disrupt my sleep at night.

Still, despite your best efforts to stay healthy and happy there may be times when you need a break. I once worked with a woman who never took breaks. The school that we worked at offered periodic vacation breaks for time off during the school year, but this particular teacher chose to offer "day care" to the parents during every one of these breaks because she wanted extra money. That is all good, but as a result of never allowing herself time off she was one of the most angry teachers that I've ever worked with. She screamed at the children, at other teachers, snapped at people during staff meetings, etc. I had to wonder if her disposition would have been improved if she had just taken some time off occasionally.

It's important to feel rejuvenated and to do this spiritual people especially need to give time to themselves that rejuvenates the energy. Spiritual people, after all, nurture other people and the world regularly to help heal it so it is vital that you realize that to avoid burnout you have to also nurture yourself. When doing spiritual practices it's important to take the time to absorb what is happening within you, to contemplate and to reevaluate. This replenishes your Shakti or spiritual energy.

However, while working in any career choice if you are burned out, acknowledge this. Reaching the point of burnout does not make you a "bad" person. You are human and you have to take care of yourself. It may be good to take a summer off to go somewhere occasionally or even a year long sabbatical to just be you. When you return to your every day work life you will feel better and will be able to give more of yourself to the people who you care for in your job.

Become aligned with your inner being and you will always know what is needed. When you do this you will stay healthy and you become aware of what are your needs. When we consider what our needs are we often acknowledge that a goal of life may be to attain a certain position whether in a career, relationship or a spiritual pursuit. This goal, however, can only be met when healthy, in-tune with ourselves and when we are grounded.

This pursuit can unconsciously spark something within us when we meet someone for the first time. This smiling person saying all the right things probes us to want something that she or he represents. This can inspire us, however, often this desire leads to hurtful envy if not checked.

The pretty woman who has only done sweet things for you pushes your buttons and makes you reactive. Despite her kindness you nitpick. First, you say hurtful things and then backstab, undermine and go out of your way to cause her harm. She never saw it coming and you don't understand it yourself, however, there is something about her that you either want *for* yourself or dislike *within* yourself. The clue to this mystery is "*you.*" When you look into the eyes of this person you have to see your *own* mirror.

What is being triggered in you?

Once I had a coworker who was loud. She was so boisterous that other people called her, "Obnoxious." She laughed heartily, talked so that everyone in the building could overhear her conversations and seemed **never** to be quiet.

When I *met* her, however, I liked her. I enjoyed what I perceived as "cheerfulness" though this changed soon afterward because it felt that she stomped around throwing punches at everyone energetically. As a result I guarded myself around her. This worked for a while until I became her target. Did I handle this well? Not at all. I threw the punches right back and it wasn't attractive, but then I looked inward to see what was really going on because things are rarely as they appear.

I realized that I not only felt drained around this person, but I also felt pushed out of the circle of visibility because her energy consumed. I realized how strong my own ego need to be seen as part of the team was and that this was the "position" that I wanted to hold onto. I saw too how this had permeated into a battle of who was the stronger and more influential. When I realized this I let it go through the tool of detachment. I detached myself from the energy of this person and from my own ego need to be seen as an individual.

At first, this was an "exercise" that I had to work on and then it became easeful. It was blissful because my ego no longer prompted the demand to be acknowledged. I smiled more, laughed easier and when things came up I let them go not because I was resigned, but because I no longer needed to get into that battle of punches to be **recognized**. Ironically, I felt more room in my own heart when the outer space no longer held importance and I felt compassion for my former boxing mate coworker as well as for myself.

Take care of the spiritual person that is you and you will have an amazing life!

Perfection Through Contentment

Yesterday I sat at the pool to write in my journal when my concentration was interrupted by a little boy's incessant chattering to someone who was not responding. The child repeated several times, "I can do **better** than she can! I'm **faster** than she is! Can't you see! I can do **more** than she can!"

I won't deny that I wanted him to **shut up** because he was interrupting *my* peace, but he continued, "I'm **better** than she is!" His parent ignored his commanding retorts and didn't seem the slightest bothered by the loudness. I wondered if I had lost the patience that I've had with children and then I realized that it was more than the noise that troubled me. I was being triggered by what was being said.

My mother taught us not to "Show off." She told us that we didn't *need* that kind of attention and that it was "wrong" to "Toot your own horn." As I grew I became quiet, shy and reserved. I held fear instead of joy. This manifested itself with me sitting in the back of classrooms, being alone and certainly not drawing attention to myself. I learned to live vicariously while my classmates bragged about their adventures.

Still, as time went on and I became a woman I realized that I was living in the shadows of people who I admired and loved. Why was I taking a back seat? Why did I do that to myself, and yes, *I* did this to myself; no one else did this to me, but me. I had to look at this and with the help of my spiritual teacher I began to go deeper into why it was that I felt the need to hide.

My spiritual teacher said to me, "You wear fear like a shield." Wow! What a thing to say, huh? It was very powerful and something that I've never forgotten.

When I looked at this I saw too that most people are afraid to shine. We don't want to look bad. We don't want to come across as braggarts either. The little boy at the pool shouldn't have the need or care that he is "better than" whoever "she" is. He instead should feel content with who *he* is and with what *he* can do and not the need to compare himself to others. Sound familiar?

Contentment which stems from deep within us elicits our joy. This joy is our own and no one can take it from us regardless of how well they do or how poorly we do. When we are steady in that place of contentment it no longer matters what someone else is doing because we are at peace within ourselves. No one can out shine us, make us feel small or outdo us because we know our own greatness and this is our real and true power.

Is there a little boy who lives inside you that calls out that you can do better than another? In the end, we can't control how well or what another person does and sometimes we can't even control how well we do, but we can control our acceptance and love for ourselves regardless.

I think that this takes God's grace and it also takes introspection and contemplation. We need to be able to look at what comes up when it comes up to delve deep into our triggers. For me, detachment is also a great tool. I'm not always good at it, but when I remember and return to it I'm better off because I'm able to go back to that joyful place that is within me and that *is* me. In my own contented heart when that little girl's voice calls out, "She's better than you" I am able to laugh.

There will always be people who are better than I am at certain things, but no one is better than I am and no one is better than you are. We are equally great and all that we have to do is believe this. As a teacher I often saw the kind of behavior that this little boy displayed in my classrooms and had to contemplate the issues at hand as well as my own personal resolutions within me before reacting. When you come across a child bragging and calling attention to himself what do you do? Do you try to shut the child up? Do you ignore or do you attempt to help that child to see that he is perfect? When we see the children as perfect we are able to teach them that they don't need to compete and when we don't need to compete our lives are led with contentment because we know who we are. We are secure in this knowledge and we can offer this to the world because we are at home within our own skin.

Consider the lessons given in The Wizard Of Oz. On her journey toward "Home" Dorothy followed the lead of others and sought the advice of the "wise." She was in awe of the beauty around her and she enjoyed the company of those who she loved, but was never content as she strove to get to that always in the horizon, "Home."

I'm a lot like Dorothy.

When I was a little girl I *felt* old and isolated. Still, I was a child who loved more than anything else to run through tall sweet smelling grass. This made me happy, and yet, I sought a place to *feel* at home (completely at ease). I knew that this place was there in that field of poppies though fear held me back and left me discontent. Where was "Home" and why couldn't I *get* "there?"

As I traveled through life I was helped by my elders including parents, siblings, teachers, aunts, uncles and friends. I was advised, counseled and steered in certain directions. This assistance though heartfelt left me with an uncertainty about my own power of decision making. It was as if that yellow brick road which led to my own authority was undermined because I sought *outward* advice.

Like Dorothy, I was a bit of a free spirit although the adults around me sometimes hovered. I *knew* that the journey toward "Home" was worth it because it would eventually lead me to freedom.

The tornado that knocked me on the head and spun me into new directions came after my parents died. At thirty, I lost my "Auntie Em" though suddenly had a sense of freedom that I had never known and this put me in the direction of a Wizard only my Wizard unlike Dorothy's was/is **powerful**.

The enormous greatness of this Wizard shook me to the core literally and I knew that this being would take me "Home." At last, the yellow brick road would lead me to that place that I had sought since I was a child.

Remember in the Wizard of Oz when Dorothy recognized the greatness of her friends? She turned to the Scare Crow and said, "You are smarter than anyone that I know." She told the Tin Man, "You have **biggest** heart!" She reminded the Cowardly Lion of his many feats of bravery. She saw the goodness in those around her, but what did she forget?

She forgot that all of these qualities that she so admired in her friends were also within herself.

Still, evil followed her causing disasters wherever she went. Dorothy's evil manifested as a "Wicked Witch," but don't we all have some form of that "Wicked Witch" who challenges our decisions? We get tripped up by this "Wickedness" when we don't listen to our own intuition and forget our own hearts. We get **scared** and we take the wrong paths which lead to bad choices for our lives.

However, just like Dorothy we also have the "good witch" to steer us to the right direction and remind us that, "There's no place like Home." As she did with Dorothy, Glenda (the "Good Witch") never leaves us. She smiles at us and shows us her unconditional love. Glenda is the heart and she is always within us as us.

As our hearts, Glenda points each of us to our own path and shows us the way to the Wizard within. Yet, many of us struggle to find our path and we fight with our Wizard. This is because our egos (our "Wicked Witches") are insecure. The ego blinds us to our way "Home." Just like the "Wicked Witch" did to Dorothy the ego makes us forget that "Home" is inside us. Thankfully, Glenda doesn't give up on us. She is our goodness. She is our love and our wisdom. She is the intuition and when we learn to listen to her instead of the ego the path to "Home" comes easily.

I'm a lot like Dorothy and sometimes it takes a whirlwind to hit me on the head for me to get back to that place within, but I do get there. How about you? Have you found your way "Home?"

If not, what's stopping you? Think about it.

Children are more openhearted and minded than most adults and see the world as adventurous: wondrous. They see the world as perfect. Do you remember that feeling of "awe?" It was as if the sky, clouds and trees had a world all their own which they allowed you to take part in.

In that "awe" there was a connection with the Universe that supported you with no boundaries. In this you heard the voice of God within you as you. It was your intuition and it's never left you though often it's not heard.

Listen to the voice within you and you will move into the heart which connects us all. It is the voice of love; the voice of God. When we listen to that voice we know that everything and everyone is perfect. When we have this recognition we are able to allow other people to be who they are without our judgements and restrictions. Everyone in your life is then free to make their own mistakes, experiment, play and be themselves as they grow and develop with our blessings of their internal perfection.

Have you noticed that often children are enthusiastic and able to see the perfection in all, yet, somehow as they grow and "mature" they lose this? As adults, we become jaded, cynical and afraid to trust. We no longer see the rainbows at the end of the journeys that we trail. We only see dust and feel sweat on our brows because we're ingrained in our difficulties rather than the adventure of life.

Somewhere in time we are taught to be "Careful" and this eventually makes us feel afraid instead of perfect.

I'm not saying that being *careful* is a bad thing. I think that it's important to use your discrimination so that you make good decisions and to keep good company. Toxic people can make you sick literally.

However, often we get so caught up in being *cautious* that we forget the joy that is life itself. For example, several years ago I taught in a school during an El Ninyo year which means that it rained constantly. I taught young children who only wanted to go outside. We decided to make a big bucket of bubble solution and told the parents to dress the children in rain gear. We got out bikes and rode to a nearby park where there was an awning and where we played with the bubbles. Sure, we got wet, but no one melted and we had fun. A few years later I suggested this plan in another school where I taught but the owner balked. She said, "But...the kids...they'd get *wet!* Parents would *complain!* Oh **NO!**" *sigh* Her fear dictated her decisions.

Fear can be a protective instinct. There are children who climb the tallest structures as if monkeys and others who hold back. I never push them. They whisper, "I'm scared" and I tell them to listen to that little voice which is there for a reason. It keeps us safe and guides us.

That voice is your intuition. It is the God within you. You should always honor it.

The voice that dictates worry, however, is far from your intuition. It does not allow you to participate in life's abundance. It nags at you and harbors illusions of distress, fret and agitation. This is the ego. It's goal is to shame and scare you. It holds you back from your true potential and from your happiness.

Have you ever made decisions when afraid? How did that work for you? You may have decided to take a specific job or have done something only because you were afraid. Due to fear you jumped. In my life, this has rarely if ever worked out well for me and has often led to disasters. I've learned through this kind of mistake to become a witness to my fears. I am not at a place (yet) where I am totally fearless, but I know now to allow the fear to come up, look at it and to witness it without jumping into it. I've found that when I can make this mediation on my fears a practice whatever is "Scary" for me dissipates and only then can I make decisions for myself that are successful for my life.

It's not easy to place yourself in a position of the "Witness" when fear eats at your heart though there are ways to help yourself. I go for long walks and look at the birds in flight as somehow their ability to soar through the sky helps me. I pray. I also sometimes use my imagination as a guide. For instance, I will picture myself sitting on a cloud above the world to distance myself from the worries and in doing this

I am able to see the issues more clearly than I can when engrossed in fear. I also write in my journal, take long baths and allow myself the time to contemplate. How about you? What do you do to help yourself when fear is knocking at your door?

How do you discern from a fear-based voice from that of God's? Meditate. Go inward and listen to your heart. You will find the long lost joy that you held in spades as a child regardless of lifestyle. I say this because I've seen children who have come from horrific backgrounds and still there is that enthusiasm for life itself. You can have it too when you get to know *you*. God's voice is never one of fear and instead is one of reason and clarity.

When we let go and let be we allow the children within us and the physical children in our lives the possibilities of adventure without restriction which is elicited by fear. We make the right decisions for ourselves and we TRUST in the process.

Staying in the Present Moment

Most of us have expectations for ourselves, others and from life, but what if just for a moment we let go and lived in the present moment? What would life look like if we allowed ourselves the freedom to just "be?"

Like most of us I grew up with expectations. Mine was a family of boys with older parents who expected differently from and for the boys than they did me and this elicited perceptions for our lives.

For instance, my old fashioned parents encouraged my brother to drive earlier than they did me and when we dated they had no problem when his girl friend spent nights at our house while it was strictly forbidden for me to spend the night with a man much less invite him to spend nights at our house. My parents hovered over me and when they retired set my brother up in an apartment while I was told that I was not "ready" to be on my own.

My brother's perception was that he was tossed to the wind while I was "lovingly" held onto. *My* perception was that he was considered "capable" and I "incompetent." In turn, my brother got married young. He created his own family which provided him a sense of security that he didn't have when younger and I became maybe too fiercely independent because while doing this I closed myself off from relationships. My expectation of myself was to make it on my own without help from anyone as if a need to prove competence. This was my karma to work out which was unlike that of my brother's.

We come into our lives with lessons to learn and our tribulations teach us the most. Ultimately, expectation from how we were raised or from the world leads to struggle. However, our perceptions have the power to shape the outcome of our lives. What we think and hold onto as our realities manifests into our lives because our thoughts are powerful. They magnify into the Universe and create the world that we live in.

If instead of holding onto expectation, we surrendered to the present moment we would have no worry, judgment, struggle or fear. We would live in freedom instead of the mind's trappings.

Consider the greatest beings in time from Jesus, Gandhi to Mother Teresa and how they lived without expectation for reward. They were able to come from their hearts because they were centered in an awareness that is beyond that of the ego.

Most of us hold these figures of greatness as beyond ourselves, but truthfully the awareness that they lived in is what they wanted for all of us. It is their gift to us and it is within all of us.

How can we achieve this? The way to the awareness of the heart that is always within the present moment and free from struggle is through meditation.

Begin by becoming aware of the simplicity of your surroundings. Close your eyes and listen to whatever is there. This can be anything including cars, people, music, birds, and allow yourself to go deeper into your own body. Simply be aware of how your body is feelings whether cold, warm tired, hungry, frustrated, etc., and sense your breath go in and out naturally with ease and without expectation. Within this space delve deeper into the cavity that is your body and feel your heart's beat. This is the pulsation of the Universe and it is within you. Rest in this space.

When I come to this awareness within me as me I am able to come from love because in this place I have no sense of mistrust for myself or from others. In this awareness, I am free because there is no sense restraint or ironically of expectation. It is beyond the ego which holds all judgment, fear and thoughts of lack. It is pure.

Energetically life is moving quickly presently. This can be stressful and can provoke expectations. Be patient and compassionate with yourself and with others and go within the heart of you. Reside in this place within you because when you are in that state that is all your own greatness you can create, build upon and allow for a life that is ultimately free.

Once while my second grade teacher lectured about family life I yawned and escaped to daydream land. Unfortunately for me, however, the teacher noticed and called on me. "Marian, what would you feed...?" I shook myself out of that other realm and answered with assuredness, "Well, dog food, of course..." The whole class burst into laughter. The conversation that began with a discussion about the family's *dog* had changed to one of the family's *baby*. Whoops!

Daydreaming was my outlet to relieve everyday stress for a long time and I didn't dismiss this habit easily. For me, it was like Scarlett O'Hara who said, "I will think about *that* tomorrow..." This was my mode of operation when struggling with geometry, family stuff, conflicts with friends, money worries, you name it. This was how I dealt with stress.

My tendency was to perseverate on worry so I daydreamed to escape. The issues, however, escalated because I didn't face them much less work on them. I didn't know then that the *mind* was my greatest obstacle.

When I was very young (maybe three) I had a reoccurring nightmare. My family lived in Manhattan in a two bedroom apartment which my grandmother shared with us. She slept in one bedroom and my three brothers and I in the other while my parents slept in the living room. The beds were lined up literally. It was crowded, but on the positive never lonely. In the dream, however, I woke up in my bed alone in a tin can room surrounded by steel walls while I screamed for my mother, "Mommy, Mommy!" I called and yelled, but only heard the echo of my own voice.

Growing up I had many chase and falling nightmares. The worst though came when I was a young teen. I had **horrid** reoccurring nightmares that I was possessed by Satan-- thanks to the lovely Catholic Church which often does young girls no favors. I paced in my room until dawn for months unable to sleep due to these nightmares. I didn't know then that it was my mind that created the dreamscapes which **terrified** me.

The Hindus often call the mind the "Second heart."

Practices such as meditation, contemplation, self inquiry, journaling, detachment and present orientation create a journey to self awareness and have changed my life. When working with these tools the seeker learns to go deeper than the mind's imagined fears to where the thoughts and feelings are derived instead of sweeping them under the rug as I did with daydreaming. This can be excruciatingly painful, and yet, it creates an awareness which elicits detachment and elicits healing.

I am now *present* with my life. I am in-tune with *every* moment as it happens rather than with worry about what *could* happen. My mind is focused. This is peaceful. It also creates the joy of fulfillment and even of *attainment*.

Come to think of it, I haven't had a *nightmare* in years.

However, I pay attention to my dreams. I believe that dreams give insights just as feelings do. I watch my feelings knowing that I am not my feelings. I witness them from a detached state. I can laugh about myself now. I can see my mistakes and so on as petty without *feeling* that I am "little." I can see my Self as great regardless of what I *feel*. I can see you in the same state despite what you do or say.

I pay attention to the "now" moments and this has made all the difference in my life. I love my dreams which occur only at night and I love my life issues or not.

However, it's hard to stay in the present moment when the reality is that we live in difficult times. Many of us complain about what is wrong with our country, for instance, given the continued lack of health care for all, the tax system with loop holes for the wealthy, the cost of education and so on. Yet, there is much to be thankful for.

This morning directly after my early meditation I fell back to sleep and had a flying dream. I've had these before and haven't always loved them because they ended with free falling. Scary. However, in *this* dream I had an urge to fly, but resisted because of that fear of falling, yet, somehow *had* to embrace my ability to soar. I looked to the sky, went onto my tippy toes and off I went above the clouds and through others. It was amazing, but my arms were loaded down from my purse and a shopping bag of shoes that I had bought making the flight awkward until I heard my spiritual teacher whisper, "Just let it go...Let it **all** *go*..."

I dropped my bags and my hands touched the softest cloud. I laughed and touched another one causing it to break into tiny *beautiful* pieces. The flight was blissful and when I landed unlike in previous dreams with the terrifying free falling I came back to my bed where I sat safely.

I sat there until I realized that people were in my living room moving furniture **in**. Years ago when I first met my teacher I had reoccurring dreams that my home was burglarized. I'd wake up to see the burglars removing the last of my things, but this morning these strangers were **adding** furniture! What's more, it was gorgeously decorated with sheer elegance. I was torn between yelling at the men to remove the furniture, "I **didn't** order these things and I'm **not** paying for them" and being in awe of the beauty that surrounded me.

Isn't this what most of us tend to do? Instead of allowing the beauty around us to shine through and simply going with the flow we resist, stomp our feet and cast our protests. We forget what our ancestors went through to create a government where there is freedom for everyone. We forget what those before us had to do so that we could fly freely. We forget our courage when because of our fear of falling we hold ourselves back from ever allowing that amazing flight to take place.

A few weeks ago I talked on the phone with one of my cousins about what my father and his siblings endured while growing up as Irish immigrants; physical and sexual abuse, negligence and disregard. They went through **hell**. Yet, they fought in wars as young adults for our country and became New York City police officers who protected. They were fathers who loved and later adoring grandfathers and this is our blood.

We have their perseverance, dedication and strength as their gifts to us.

Presently, there are many things that need changing in this country and we can disagree on what these are and how they need to be altered, but I think that we can all agree that there is also a great deal to be grateful for.

We have the gift to make changes, vote, become educated, choose where we want to live and who we want to love. We have freedoms.

Growing Older and Facing Death

When I was a freshman in college I contemplated joining a sorority. This idea was elicited mainly because I was new to the school and wanted to meet people, but....

At first, the group of women whom I met seemed ever so sweet, pretty and fun to be around that I was excited when they accepted me into the group of "Candidates." That excitement lasted for a few weeks until I experienced the hazing ritual which was called, "Walking The Line." This consisted of lining up in front of the "senior" sorority members so that they could yell at us and make us do stupid things until the wee hours of the mornings. I hated it and decided then that I was no longer interested in being a "sorority sister."

What if your whole life consisted of "walking the line?" To do this you'd have to follow expectations and most of the time they would not be of *your* making. You'd literally fall into patterns and your life would become mundane, boring and predictable. I knew at eighteen that this was not the life that I wanted for myself, and yet, certainly to a degree this has developed. I look back now and wonder how did that happen.

I just watched a very sweet, tear-jerker of a movie called, "The Time Traveler's Wife." It was very romantic and most definitely a "chick flick," but it got me wondering what it be like to be able to go back in time. Would we change things if we knew what was going to happen next?

Just think about it.

My mother died a month after my thirtieth birthday. As sad as this made me I've always thought that this was purposeful because she did her job with me which was to raise me to adulthood. She did what she needed to with me and then moved on, but the reality is that most people have their parents for a lot longer than I did. What if I could go back in time to when my mother was thirteen to advice her not to smoke? Back in those days even adults didn't have the knowledge that we do now about the dangers of cigarette smoking much less do young teenagers. At thirteen, my mother thought that cigarettes made her look "cool and sophisticated." What if I had the option to tell her that they'd kill her and leave her daughter without her way too soon? Would she have decided not to take that first cigarette to her lips?

What if I could tell someone else not to get into that car first thing in the morning? And another someone else not to marry that man because he'll break your heart?

Still, would I even want to tell other people what to do? No. We all have our own minds which help us to consider our choices regardless. We also all have our own karma which needs to be resolved through our choices.

However, what if I could time travel to my *own* younger days and tell myself something or other? What if I could tell myself not to spend too much time with this man because he isn't the right one or this hope and dream isn't going to manifest so don't waste your time with this? Or even "have that child now because you will stop having the ability younger than most" and "buy that house now because the economy is going to change and you won't be able to later."

Part of me would love to have the opportunity to make changes that have already occurred which ultimately would open or close a door to my life and hopefully increase happiness. Another part of me thinks that life is about change and that nothing is *stagnant*. That part of me knows that nothing lasts forever anyway and is not hell bent on holding onto anything. That part of me is flexible and resilient. Nothing is perfect *or* perhaps everything in reality is perfect if we allow it just to *be* and see the good in it regardless.

Movement. Life is full of movement, transition and change.

Take a deep breath.

I believe that we can go back and forth in time and that it's only the mind that holds us back.

What do you think?

We live in a time where women are regarded with less esteem when past a "certain age." Women of a particular time of life are labeled with names like, "Cougar" which some say is supposed to be a "compliment." This sounds predatory to me, how about you? Who by golly made up this term? Was it a man who felt guilty because he was attracted to the still stunning mature woman or was it a younger woman who felt threatened by her senior sister?

Let's get real. Many women are obsessed with how they look to the degree that they turn to plastic surgery. Look at many female older movie stars and it becomes painfully clear that going under the knife for eternal youth is the norm presently. It's sad to see a woman who was once obviously beautiful now look alien because of her efforts to remain "youthful." Due to their fame celebrities cast a realm of glamour about this kind surgery, but it's becoming popular within the mainstream also. I know a woman who claims to be in her mid-forties though has admitted to at least one "face lift." Regardless, she doesn't look forty or fifty, but appears to be in her late sixties and who knows if she would have looked better if she had allowed herself to age with dignity instead of fakery.

What happens to a woman when she starts to get older? Does she begin to fade into oblivion because her looks are not as fabulously stunning as they were when she was nineteen? How do we define the word, "Older?" How do *you* define the word, "Old?"

When men reach forty they become "middle aged," their hair begins to grey at the temples and they buy a new convertible car. Women still eye them because they look just as "cute" as they did twenty years ago and maybe even cuter, right? The grey in his hair just makes him look more sophisticated and the lines on his face make him look wiser, but take a look at his wife and do you say the same things about her.

She exercises daily and is in great shape that is "for someone her age..." "She dresses okay "for an older woman..." However, she better start to dye her hair because she's looking kinda matronly and those lines around her eyes remind me of grandma. "Did you notice that she was flirting with her daughter's boyfriend? What a Cougar!"

We have different standards for appropriate behavior and even for what is appealing for men than we do for women of certain ages, don't we?

I sat in a car one day a while back with a couple of other women. I was the youngest in that particular group and I'm not in my twenties. To be specific, one woman was in her sixties, another in her fifties and I in my forties. I've known both of these women for years and still find both attractive. The oldest was someone who I looked up to when I was growing up. I thought of her as stunning. On this day, she was distraught about having been passed up for a job promotion which was given to a woman in her twenties whom she had trained. She said that her boss "Thinks with his dick!" Secretly, I was glad that my own boss is female, but I tried to assure her of her beauty and she replied, "Beauty is not the same at sixty-two as it is at twenty-seven." "Of course not!" I said. It's not the *same*, but does that make it *less* than?

Quite frankly it's not just beauty that seems to diminish as we "mature."

We live in a society where both children and old people are dismissed. In fact, we live in a society where old people are often hidden away. We don't *want* to see them. We don't want to even think about them.

Why is that? Do they scare us? We don't want to look like them. We don't want to sound like them. We don't want their money worries and we certainly don't want their health problems. What about their wisdom and life experiences?

We call them, "Old bat!" "Hag!" "Old bitty!" We meet an older gentleman for the first time and call him, "Gramps!"

We're disrespectful of the aged, but why?

Still, I know a man who is now in his sixties. He is married to a woman right around his own age and is dating a woman in her twenties. Right on, bro, huh? Show me the man who wouldn't want to date a woman twenty, thirty or even forty years his junior. He's sophisticated with his grey hair, he's professional, successful and mature. He's got it all. How about his wife? She's attractive and successful, right? So, how come it is that if they were to divorce, he'd probably marry that twenty-something and she'd probably never marry again?

Where do you stand? Should an older woman be content with being discounted while her "mate" is not only acknowledged but held in high esteem with his "maturity?" When does a woman become a "Cougar?" Why is it okay for men to seek younger women, yet, when women are attracted to men even slightly younger they are considered "Cougars?"

The very title of "Cougar" sounds predatory. Women can no longer have children after a certain age, and yet, men can have babies at ninety. I sometimes think that men want young women because of fertility. It's all about keeping up the species, right?

Or maybe it's just the male ego...

Growing older is not easy, but who said that it would be, right?

When I was a child I watched TV with my mother and Jacqueline Bisset was shown. My mother said with an awe, "She's *so* beautiful!"

Bisset with her high cheek bones and "good" features is by all standards classically beautiful. Did you notice that I said "is" and not "was?" She "is" beautiful and she is sixty-four years old. More impressive is that in these days of plastic surgery and Botox Ms. Bisset has **never** gone under the knife and she has never been injected with Botox.

The other day she appeared on the TV show, "The View" and said that she has "never known anyone to look better" after having had these procedures. Her goal she maintained is to age gracefully.

My mother may have remarked about Jacqueline Bisset's beauty over thirty years ago, but truthfully I find her more stunning now. I also think of her as a role model. I hope that I can grow older gracefully which doesn't mean that I think that it's okay for me to lose my looks when I get older.

Yesterday, while at the grocery store I had to stop myself from staring at a woman. This woman was obviously an "older lady." She was probably closer to seventy than forty, and yet, was still strikingly attractive. She had beautiful features that we all admire; amazing cheek bones, big eyes, thick, lovely hair, etc., that continued regardless of aging. Her silver hair was styled and hit beyond her shoulders. She wore fashionable black trousers and a black blazer. She had little lines around her mouth that indicated that once upon a time she probably smoked cigarettes, but other than that she was more stunning than any twenty year old that I personally know.

Plastic surgery, Botox, Breast implants, liposuction, on and on may be what are considered "needed" these days as woman grow age, but this is not a reality.

It may be unique presently to grow older naturally, but this is my intention.

I look to women who are my senior sisters like Jacqueline Bisset and others who are proudly maturing naturally yet are still beautiful.

I think that we can all do this by taking care of ourselves with good nutrition, exercise, moisturizers, vitamins, drinking water, getting enough sleep and with meditation.

Meditation is good for the circulation which is good for the skin. If you want to age naturally and look good, meditate!

Dance to your own internal beat, be happy with who you are, meditate, take care of yourself and you will look great at any age!

As I get older I contemplate what I once wrote in my journal, "Everyone who I love the most leaves me."

I don't necessarily hold this true now, yet, rereading it makes me sad. I lost both of parents to cancers, my best friend to Ulcerative Colitis, a man that I loved, my grandmother, etc.

Death felt like the ultimate remover of love.

Yesterday, I interviewed for a job in a senior citizen center. It was a group interview though with only two candidates. My "competition" was a twenty-five year old woman who smiled at the elderly residents and spoke to them in a cheerleader voice while ignoring me. I'm not at the same stage of life that she or they are in. I'm in the middle with no desire to go backwards though trepidation about old age. Frankly, sometimes the thought of becoming *old* scares me enough to prefer death.

My career has been with the opposite spectrum; I've been a teacher with young children for most of my life. However, the interviewer said that the elderly are like children in that they have tantrums. Children act out because they don't have words, can't get their bodies to move in desired ways, are impulsive, etc. I can only imagine how challenging it must be for an elderly person who can no longer move quickly, see clearly or be as expressive as they were in the past. Perhaps the latter is more frustrating because in the case of the child there is improvement seen while the adult's capabilities decrease.

Loss comes in heavy doses as faculties, independence, skillfulness, friends, lovers, family, etc., fade away. Yet, life's cycle is unavoidable.

Accounts from Drs. Carolyn Myss, Andrew Weil and Mehmet Oz hold that with exercise, meditation and good eating habits we don't necessarily have to go down the same roads of our grandparents and that attitudes play the biggest role. We all know that if we worry, it shows on our faces. It also causes us to age poorly. It robs us of our immune system's ability to fight off carcinogenic toxins, etc.

Sleep is said to also ease the aging process. We live in a society where we run from morning to night working and then doing errands on the weekends. When do we have time for sleep? Yet, sleep benefits our cognitive processes as well as builds our immunity.

Dr. Caroline Myss says that it is possible to live to be 140! She quotes *Dr. C. Norman Shealy who ascertains that our bodies are energy which does not age. He further says that "energy is a conscious substance that requires our attention." This makes aging "self-empowering" as we come to know our "untapped potential" which he states can slow down the aging process with our own self-esteem.

When I read things like this I no longer feel fear because I don't see myself as a little old woman walking with a cane. Instead I see a powerful and wise crone. How about you? How do you see yourself when old?

Death is not a topic that many people feel comfortable with. We hear of someone's dying and we put our heads down to whisper, "I'm sorry..." We don't know what else to say and walk away in an awkward silence. Death is rarely embraced in our culture and most people, are afraid of its coming. We don't know what to expect. We've been taught about the old man with the long beard who sits in judgment of our "sins." Death often feels scary, and yet, death is part of everyone's life. It is an ingredient that we can't leave out of life's baking project...

My father had been a practicing Catholic and with that came much guilt. Frankly speaking some of this remorse was earned. Yet, there is something sad when one's religion causes a person to feel blameworthy. In my father's case, his religion seemed to profit from the production of trepidation.

Truthfully, my father had much that he regretted when he died. He apologized to me and I forgave him, but I knew that his own hell on earth had been to live with his misgivings. My father adamantly believed that when he died he would go to Purgatory due to his sins. This belief, conversely never seemed to be one of comfort and he asked my brothers and I to pray for his soul so that he could one day reach Heaven's gates.

I didn't share my father's sentiments about the need for prayer or about Purgatory. I wasn't sure about Heaven, but to appease my father I promised that I would say the prayers that he wanted to hear. I agreed and then I forgot... completely... I didn't do this out of malice. I honestly didn't see the importance in this and simply forgot...

My father died when I was thirty. He died eight months after my mother died and they both died from cancers.

My mother had been my father's "rock." Literally, this is what she was known as, "The rock…" It was a good sentiment for my mother. She was strong willed, bright, determined, stubborn and seemingly unbreakable. The truth of the matter was that she put up with a lot from my father; more than I would ever put up with from any man. This made me wonder if she put up with so much because she really loved him or because she was afraid that financially she couldn't make it without him. I think, however, that she desperately loved him…

About a year after she died I had a dream. In the dream I was swimming naked in the ocean at night in what looked like Hawaii. It was beautiful and warm. I love the ocean so for me this was as close to Heaven as one could get. I've read also that theories say that the ocean is a symbol for the great Self--or the soul. It is also said that if one can surrender to the waves, one can be with God. However, if you fight the waves, you are only battling with your own ego and you won't get anywhere…The challenge is to simply surrender.

In the dream I was at peace in the water. Still, something suddenly changed because my mother was astonishingly also swimming in the water. In life, my mother, unlike me, was not a swimmer. We swam together for a while and then she said, "You have to go! You are not supposed to be here--not yet!" She shuffled me out of the water and we ran into what looked like a hotel. There she placed a large beach towel over my still undressed body and said, "I am here in Heaven and I am waiting for your father..."

It was just a dream...or was it?

More astonishingly maybe a year later one night before falling asleep I began to think about my father. I felt sad for him because of his need for us to pray for him. I also felt a little guilt because I hadn't said even one prayer for him... I hoped too that I would feel more at peace when it became my own time for death and I began to pray--for my father. I wasn't sure really what to pray, but I prayed that he be taken care of, safe and find his way to God. With that I fell asleep.

I woke up in the middle of that night and saw something phenomenal. I saw what I believe are angels! That's right-- angels! They were not tiny cupid type of beings either. These were human sized with huge white wings and they flew around my bedroom. I sat up in my bed and watched mesmerized. I couldn't believe what I was seeing as well as hearing. They soared through the space within my small room wings flapping--loudly!

I know that this sounds rather incredible because it was and no I was not dreaming! I was visited by angels that night-- the night that I had prayed about my father! That's right--I was visited by angels on the night that I prayed about my father... I think that the angels came to me to ease my mind and let me know that he is okay--regardless...

The deaths of my parents profoundly effected me. I learned through watching my mother's death to surrender to those waves. I learned through my father's death to pray. Through these deaths I learned how to die and what is more important at least presently how to live.

They say that children are more open and I believe this. I work with children and when I see them just gazing off I sometimes wonder…what are or who are they looking at…

When I was about eight I, too felt that I was able to "see" things which other people didn't or couldn't see. One such experience occurred during the nights when I often woke up to see a beautiful woman standing by the door of my bedroom. I remember that she was slender and wore a red robe with a long scarf gently around her hair. Her eyes held an intensity. They were large, dark and almond shaped. I remember feeling that this "lady" could speak with her eyes.

I remember laying in bed while I watched her as she walked into my bedroom to sit at the edge of my bed. I watched and she stroked my hair and my hands without spoken words. I remember that my heart beat very hard though she smiled at me.

This happened nightly for a few years. I told my mother about this experience and she said that I more than likely had been dreaming. I asked my grandmother about this experience. She too thought that I must have been dreaming… Finally, I asked my brother who shared the room with me if he had seen her and to my surprise he said that he did see her. He watched her as I did but she never approached him.

In my childhood innocence I called her, "My lady…" My parents continued to say that I had been "Dreaming," but I never agreed with this conclusion. I didn't know who she was but her visitations felt special and I called her, "My lady…"

I have not had such an experience in many years, but I remember her still… "my lady"…

I don't know if there are such things as "ghosts" though I experienced a visitor at one time who I know wasn't human in the form that you or I are.

When just out of college and on my own for the first time I sought adventure somewhat foolishly. I found a job as an advertising copywriter and my first apartment. All was great except that my apartment was in a very seedy area. Instead of listening to my intuition which in this case would have given me a healthy dose of fear I told myself that this was just "a part of living in the city…" I shared this small one bedroom apartment with another young woman and we split the rent in half. She took the large living room space and I the small bedroom. For the most part, we got along well although we had opposite schedules. My roommate was a dancer and worked at night. I left at dawn to catch a bus to get to my job. Our only point of disagreement developed when leaving for work early in the morning I found that when she had gotten back home she left the door to our apartment unlocked on several different occasions though we talked about this and she promised to be more "careful." After that we further argued when I learned that I was paying the balk of the rent which she justified because even though her room was much larger than was mine I had a "door" to my bedroom.

Mornings were always rushed for me as I often ran to catch my bus before the break of daylight. One such morning while locking the door behind me I was startled because I saw someone standing by the staircase which was next to our apartment. There stood a young man who was about the age that I was then with golden hair that was the color of my own. However, the oddest thing about him was that he was dressed in clothing that looked like he was from a much earlier century. He watched me with intensity. The potency of his eyes obviously carried a message. I turned around and gazed at him again with a certain recognition. Somehow, I felt a knowingness and had no fear of him. In fact, I felt like this was someone whom I knew well though he was not someone who I knew in this lifetime at all. I also knew immediately that he was there to warn me to leave that apartment. The problem, however, was that I was too young to be told what to do by *anyone*.

A week later someone broke into the apartment and attempted to rape my roommate while I slept in my small bedroom unaware. My roommate, the strong dancer wrestled with him and alerted him that her "roommate" would hear him. Apparently, the door that my roommate and I had argued over kept me safe as he responded with, "You don't have a roommate! This is a studio!" He then threatened her with one of our own kitchen butcher knives, yet, she managed to get away from him. She screamed loud enough to wake me and I came running only to see him dart out of the apartment.

I never spent another night there, but looking back I've always thought that the young man who I had seen by that staircase that morning had been there to protect me. He was there to warn me of the danger that came with that apartment. I don't know who he was or what he was, but I know that he came to help me…

I often hold that those people from our past lives are still with us in one form or another. I also believe that the aspirations that we've held whether these have been realized or not in this lifetime come from those that we worked on in the past.

Once upon a time I was a golden haired little girl with curls who chased after my brothers and laughed so hard that my mother called me, "Merry Annie."

As if a dream that held no nightmares life was playful and adventurous with hopes for an abundant future. Those days in upstate New York we ran through the "woods" that were our backyard, skated on thin iced ponds with boots and knew all of our neighbors. I made "mud pies" for dinners as we fielded off the "bad guys" with forks. Imagination told us that anything was possible.

Our family traveled across country to California; the land of earthquakes and movie stars. Christmas was eighty degrees and was spent swimming in our pool instead of playing in the snow. I missed my best friend, yet, there was magic in the air as I grew into a long haired and legged teenager with aspirations to write, work with animals and to someday have children of my own.

Did everything that I hope for happen? No, not really and yet kind of.

With a degree in Advertising/Journalism I worked as a reporter/photographer and then as an advertising copywriter giving me a taste of professional writing. It wasn't glamorous and it didn't take creativity. It was just 'work.' I went back to school to study education and became a teacher. I never got to be a mom, but I've taught children for most of my adult life and in a way think of myself as a mom to the world's children. I didn't become a veterinarian either though did do rescue work and have had animals throughout my life.

Did I compromise on my "Once upon a time" dreams? Absolutely, yes, I did make concessions with myself and with my God, but life isn't over yet, and, I affirm that everything happens for reasons.

Once upon a time, my teenage best friend, Loretta said, "You don't know why this happened...maybe in the future you will see that you will use the knowledge this taught you in a way that you can't see now." Loretta was a wise sixteen year old. Her words resonated then and still do because I believe that life teaches us what we need to know in mysterious ways. We grow, serve each other and become full within our highest selves through life's experiences whether "good" or not so great.

My "Once upon a time" may be a thing of the past, and yet, for another little girl it is now. When I see that little girl my dreams come alive again. In my heart, that little dreaming girl and I share hopes for life that are blessed by love.

"Once upon a time" I was a little girl and now I am a woman whose dreams have manifested into a life led by her heart.

*http://www.normshealy.com/

The Power of Forgiveness

"In order to do all that God wants you to do, you must learn how to be criticized, misunderstood, rejected and be able to forgive those who are behind it." ~ Joyce Myers

I tend to be very trusting, however, when someone betrays, belittles and rejects me I stubbornly fight forgiving. Yet, in my heart I am a highly spiritually oriented person. I want the best for humanity and to serve God.

There is a dichotomy with the need to serve God while holding resentment because in reality we are *all* of God.

Once when emotionally beaten down by another's misplaced vengeance and my own resentment I realized how my stance hurt me. I knew that I had to let go and to forgive. This is a hard lesson and one that is repeated until mastered.

When we carry anger in our hearts this energy is permeated into the Universe. It affects those who may not be as strong as we are and elicits negative reactions in a domino effect. For instance, a misunderstanding between you and your partner creates tension in the house which effects your teenage son who has been bullied at school. He then brings a gun to school to take care of those who have hurt him. The negative energy manifested has intensity with grave consequences.

Energy is powerful and our thoughts and emotions are energetic.

How can we serve God or our highest Selves when we carry negative energy that hurts humanity?

Perhaps one of God's greatest lessons is compassion. When we are able to forgive we learn compassion. With compassion we find understanding for those who have hurt us and we see them as ourselves. Although, we see the flaws that create the misunderstandings we have empathy due to our own struggles. We are each taught by our individual tests to reach deep into the heart and let go for the higher good.

Our tribulations are meant to make us stronger and to teach us about humanity. They give us resilience and the ability to see the struggles that others also go through. This insight creates a way to forge through hard times with other people and illuminates the Godliness that is within us all despite the differences between us and our challenges.

There have been people in my life that have felt "toxic" and that I have chosen to disconnect with because of the desire to "keep good company." I've learned that often our associations keep us strong or make us weak because they are influential. However, I've also learned of the power of forgiveness. These people may no longer be in my life, yet, I hold light for them. I see them in my heart as love regardless.

In this way, I am learning to forgive so that I can serve with my heart. How about you?

Perhaps one of the easiest way to hurt another person is with our words. A friend unexpectedly came over to my house late one Sunday morning. I, still in my pajamas offered her coffee before we sat in my sunny living room to "talk." She divulged that she "*had*" to tell me something. I pointed at a plush chair as she gathered her strength to disclose that *I* had been the topic of belittling gossip.

My mouth fell open but words failed me. I didn't know *what* to say. My mind raced as my heart sank. A myriad of emotions including hurt, anger and embarrassment bubbled up inside me. I wondered too *why* my "friend" felt compelled to invest in this. Did she really think that I *had* to know this? Why?

Have you been the focal point of gossip? How did it make you feel?

A few years ago I opened the school where I worked with a coworker. Each day when with this person I felt exhausted and this is why:

"Good morning, Polly! How are you?"

"I'm *okay*... Did you notice that **Emily** left the kitchen in a mess *again?*"

"*Oh*...yeah... I saw..."

"Emily is the **messiest** person! She's leaves things *everywhere*... She is *so* **lazy!**"

At first, I listened, but before I knew it I too had joined the gossip party as if this bonded Polly and I. I didn't *like* it and knew that it didn't make me feel *good* to take a part in the gossip so decided to talk to Polly about this:

"I've been thinking about how we interact lately, Polly... Perhaps in our efforts to *bond* we've indulged in gossip."

Polly sighed heavily and said, "**Well!** I **have** to be able to **VENT!**"

I continued shyly, "Maybe we could find other things to talk about because to be honest these conversations make me feel tired and dragged down..."

Polly quickly gathered her things, turned around abruptly and stormed away with obvious indignation. That went well, didn't it? Yikes!

Why is it that often the intent that we have when we gossip is to bring us together somehow, yet, the reality is that it tares us apart? I doubt that Polly enjoyed the gossip anymore than I did, and yet, she resisted ending it. Why? My take on this is that regardless of its negative connotations there is *energy* in gossip. It "Stirs the pot" and feels like "Fun" for the moment though ultimately leaves us feeling drained.

In all honesty, regardless of what was said I tend not to remember the gossip shared with me.

A friend used to call me on the phone and the first thing that she'd say was, "I have a *secret*, but you can't tell *anybody*!" Her voice was *enthusiastic* with glee. "Pssssss...." She'd spill her guts or somebody else's and I'd listen. Ironically, whatever it was that was exposed would be forgotten moments later. The facts being revealed were not as exciting as was the energy of the "Secret."

The reality is that most of us don't hang onto gossip because it's not *relevant* to *our* lives. It holds *momentary* excitement, but unless it pertains to our lives we don't *care* enough to hold onto it. Seriously, who *cares* if Emily was messy or what Brent wore to the office last Friday? Gossip in the moment can be thrilling because it elicits a sensation of superiority, but the revelations are forgettable. Gossip doesn't inspire or enlighten though it does drag us down.

Wouldn't it be great if we didn't partake in tidbits that tore apart at someone else and our own psyches but instead shared *positive* information about other people and ourselves? Have you noticed that conversations rarely go like this:

"Hey, Janet! Did you hear that Billy got an award at work yesterday?"
"That's great! He **deserves** it!"
"He's *such* a **hard** worker!"
"I'm **thrilled** that he was acknowledged!"

We rarely engage in this kind of exchange, and yet, when we do we come away **exuberant**. This is like a pat on the back not only for Billy, but for us because we've *celebrated* in each other and in our interconnections.

Words are powerful because they are energetic. Haven't you noticed that positive exchanges elicit **hope** while gossip rips it away?

Let's make a pact today not to gossip, but instead to use our prolific words with the intention to aspire and to serve and heal our world. We *can* **do** this!

Regardless, however, of our intentions it isn't easy to get along with people and there have been times in my life when I preferred isolation. I would have made a great bear who hibernated in her cave, but I wasn't born a bear at least in this lifetime so I've had to learn how to be *with* people. I think that this is a skill that most of us have had to acquire in one way or another.

I have learned much from children. Some children **love** being with others. They gravitate toward their peers with enthusiasm. Once I had a darling little boy in my classroom who poked and prodded his "friends" for attention. His tactics appeared to the other children as "teasing" although he didn't *mean* to annoy. For instance, he'd take their puzzle pieces and when they'd scream at him he'd run laughing with hopes that they'd chase after him. As far as he was concerned it was all **fun**. He wanted to *play*, but most of his peers were **not** amused with his behavior.

I've known many adults whose social skills were not much better than were this little boy's. These people also prod, tease and goad at their peers. When these people get our awareness we usually respond with anger, but even that is attention and that is what they seek.

Once there was a little girl in my classroom. She was pretty; she was very blonde and looked like the epitome of Goldilocks so the other children gravitated toward her, but *she* wanted her **space**. The other children followed her around and sat or stood as close to her as possible and she didn't know how to handle this. She screamed, pushed and finally bit just for them to **move.** I bought Hula Hoops for the classroom and used these to demonstrate how personal space gives comfort for most people. We used these toys to work on what we called our "space bubbles" so that the other children were taught not to be as intrusive as they had been with this little girl and she learned how to express her need for physical space. She *became* assertive. She stood up for herself in a healthy and non physical way which helped her to take care of her own needs. This is a great skill that many of us adults are still working on and she had it down!

I learn a lot from the children.

I had an allocation with a friend once which caused me sadness. This was elicited by a misunderstanding which created hurt feelings for both of us. Her way of handling conflicts between herself and other people was indirectness. Many times in the past she confided in me that she was "no longer speaking to" so and so. This seemed to be *her* way when angry. It *isn't* my way by a *long* shot. Truthfully, I tend to talk it out until I'm blue in the face so didn't understand my friend's approach. It felt passive aggressive and egotistical *to me*. *My* way, however, may not be the best either as I tend to blurt things out and get unnecessarily emotional. Still, I've found that even with all the feelings that are expressed there is love that is also manifested which ignites forgiveness, acceptance and even appreciation when there is communication. The trick that I aspire to is to create a way to convey my truth so that it is heard as is the other person's regardless of differences in communication styles. I believe that this takes active listening which involves taking the time to really hear the other person rather than simply jumping to assumptions. It also requires of us to speak our truths at the right time and in a way that is not hurtful. This takes discernment.

I had a coworker who was an extremely nervous person. She was demanding and I often felt **badgered** by her. Regardless, I saw her as a sweet person who I liked because I also saw in her a good heart that desired to help other people. I *admired* her kindness so when she got high strung and nervous I **reminded** myself of the person who I know her to be. Ultimately, I hope that when people see *my* faults they also remember the person who they know *me* to be.

We keep moving, growing and becoming and that is all that we can do in this adventure called living in a social world, but it's not easy, is it?

As a spiritual person what I have learned the most about allocations is that forgiveness raises vibrations. It allows for you to let go of the hurt and anger. Ultimately, when we forgive another we are ridding ourselves of the negative energy that was carried when we held onto the feud. Forgiveness is freeing!

Memories and Transitions

I remember walking home from school when I was about eight. The seasons were transitioning from winter to spring and I relished this change. I walked through a muddy pathway and took delight in the mud because this meant that the snow had melted. I was thrilled not to have to wear a heavy coat and noticed too all the flowers that were blossoming. My favorites were the pussy willows which I gathered to take home in a bouquet for my mother.

On this walk I remember thinking to myself that someday I would be a grown up. I recollected all the things that I had learned and even though I had a happy childhood I didn't want to go back in time because at that young age I had already ascertained that learning was challenging. I didn't want to have to relearn the multiplication times tables again for instance. At that moment, I was completely content with where I was in life mostly because of how loved I felt...

I remember riding in the car that August night with my parents. I sat snuggled up to my mother in the front seat with my head on her soft breast as my father drove the car. My parents spoke quietly because two of my brothers were asleep in the back seat. I listened to the sounds of their voices and looked out the window to the stars above; the stars and that man in the moon who winked at me mischievously.

I sat close to my mother and listened to the sounds of my parents' voices not caring about what was being said. I felt safe and loved.

We drove back to our little two story house in upstate New York after having gone to the town's annual summer carnival that was sponsored by the Fire Department. I had been excited about the carnival all day. It was one of those summer things that I anticipated with eagerness. The carnival went on for one whole week every summer and during that week we went there each night. It was one of those things that I could never get enough of, and yet, driving home snuggled close to my mother as I listened to the sounds of my parents' conversation I felt most safe and loved.

I watched the twinkles of the stars in the dark night time sky and thought back to how I had begged my mother to take me onto the Ferris Wheel. She hated the Ferris Wheel and said that it made it her sick so my older brother took me at least three times. We were both adventure junkies who ate too much cotton candy and rode Ferris Wheels. I snuggled closer to my mother and vowed never to forget this night and I never have.

My parents were not wealthy people and they couldn't give us many things, but they wanted for us to have the kinds of childhood memories that we would hold onto forever. For me, the carnival and the ride home is one of those that I treasure. I can even remember the clothes that I wore to the carnival; shorts and a little sleeveless top. I remember the sounds of the rides and of the neighbors who ran up ahead waving at us. I remember getting lost in the crowds, but always being able to find my way back to my parents.

Ironically, I think that the ride home was just as special as was the carnival itself and I remember thinking and hoping that I could always feel as safe and loved as I did on that night. However, life is life and I haven't always held onto those feelings of safety or of being loved, but when I'm scared or sad I go back to the times when I felt as profoundly cared for as I did on that night.

Thankfully, there have been times in my life when I have also been able to give someone else this kind of love and safety though I wish that I could do this more than I have.

Transitions in life come up all the time even when we least expect it. I find it interesting as a grown up that particular times stay in our minds like the times when I was eight has for me. Sometimes when working with children I've had the wonderment about what they would remember and what they'd forget. Somehow, when I was eight on that particular walk I knew that it would be a memory that would be banked in my mind forever along with the time that I got burned while roasting marshmallows on a campground and when my cousin and I purposefully cut our fingers to become "Blood sisters."

I'm not sure why some memories are held onto while others are relinquished in the fire of forgettability.

A few months ago as if stoked by some kind of fire memories erupted from the past. I'm not sure why at that particular time these bubbled within me to be recollected. Some were dramatic and others sweet.

I remembered that at twenty-one and in college I lived in the dorm. I spent the weekends visiting my brother who lived an hour north of my school.

To get to my brother's I walked through the campus to the downtown area which was unsavory with halfway homes, alcoholics and derelicts. I remembered not wanting to be noticed because this made me feel safer as I walked. Once downtown I took a bus to the train to get to my brother's place.

My brother lived in Berkeley and I loved it there. Somehow, when with my brother who was six years my senior I felt more sophisticated than I did normally. We were also becoming close for the first time in our lives since we were young children. We spent evenings often into the wee hours of the mornings talking and drinking wine and when it was time for me to go back to school my brother loaded me up with bottles of "good" wines to take back with me.

However, during this particular memory I carried back the wine, my backpack of clothes and an armful of books. In other words I was loaded down.

The train was crowded and I hurried to get my ticket so that I'd make my bus back to campus, but when I got to the bus stop I realized that my wallet was missing. Frantic, I searched my purse and my backpack--nope, it was **gone**... By now it was dark and I was in a downtown area that I was not familiar with and penniless. I had no way of getting back to campus. I stood at the bus stop and tried to hold myself together so that I didn't cry.

At last, the bus pulled up. The door opened up and the driver didn't glance my way as he waited for me to get in and pay my fare only I didn't have the fare or a way to pay for it. I stood there and shakily said, "Help me!" Finally, the driver looked at the young woman standing in the dark whispering, "My wallet was stolen..."

I was lucky because he smiled. He told me to get in and said, "It will be okay..." He must have taken pity on the young college girl who stood there in the night air trying her hardest not to cry. As he drove to my stop near the campus he chatted lightly smiling often and when finally at my stop he said, "Be careful out there..." It's been many years since that night and I still remember his face because in my mind his was the face of an angel.

I walked through that downtown area with the derelicts and back through the very dark campus to the dorm which was lit up even from a distance. Immediately upon entering the dorm I heard chattering noises from the students who lived there. There had been many times that I had wished that it was quieter in the dorm, but at that moment I was grateful for the sounds of laughter and gossip because I suddenly felt safe.

I went to the commissary for dinner with my roommate as if nothing had happened, but that night as I tried to sleep my mind raced back to the train where my wallet had been stolen and I tried to recollect moments in which someone came too close, but nothing. I tried to recall all faces and none stood out. This was strange because I had always been hypersensitive. I had always been almost too aware of details and of those around me, but nothing stood out in my mind that gave way to impressions.

A week later a small white envelope with no return address came to me in the mail containing my driver's license and 'Student ID' card.

I never thought that this night would be forgotten. I was terrified at the time, and yet, somehow as time went by the memory ceased to be carried.

I never thought that I would forget Isabelle either, but did until her memory resurfaced a few months ago~

I was twenty when a group of girls invited me to join them on an expedition to "help" people in halfway homes. I knew nothing of what to expect, but had seen residents from these homes wonder through the college campus. I had even witnessed one washing his hair in a campus drinking fountain. A professor sadly noted that in previous decades Reagonomics forced cutbacks on health care and this left many of those who previously lived in mental hospitals on the streets or in halfway homes. Either way, seeing this was shocking for a girl straight out of a pretty upper middle class So California suburb.

One of my friends was studying to be a Social Worker while another wanted to help because she was "Christian." I was neither religious or interested in social work, but was altruistic, young and idealistically good hearted. I joined the girls with the intention of doing "good" with my smile and helpful hands.

We took the bus from the downtown area to where this particular halfway home was located. My religious friend sat with her bible on her lap and my social worker student friend chattered on about different theories that she was studying as if to indicate what we were about to see.

The halfway home was in what appeared to be a residential area. It was a dilapidated old Victorian house that clearly once upon a time was beautiful. We entered into the kitchen where one person was standing at an old wooden table chopping cucumbers for a big salad, another stood at the stove and stirred simmering beans while another washed dishes at a sink. My social worker student friend explained why we were there and the dishwasher turned to another room to loudly shout, **"Amelia!"**

Amelia was an abrupt middle aged woman who was obviously in charge. She shook our hands and announced that she would give us a tour as if telling the residents that she would be busy. Still, her eyes glanced quickly around the room to each of the women standing there as if to micromanage their work. She suddenly waved us on and we followed her.

It was a big, two story house with a rickety staircase, but what hit me quickly was the scent of urine which permeated throughout the house and almost gagged me.

Amelia continued her tour all the while bellowing at various residents to do this or that. She came across like a drill sergeant. All the while as she did this my observant eyes took everything in from the lacy bedspreads to the people who appeared to be rushing around until at last we stopped in the main room which was like a family's living room complete with a television that residents sat watching. The shades were pulled and the only light for this room came from the television. I was surprised to see a man sitting in a lazy boy chair while a couple of women sat on the couch. I was struck too by their clothes because they were old, tattered and as if bought in previous decades. We were then "invited" to sit down. I remember not wanting to sit because of that scent which continued its lack of welcoming, but at last I sat and smiled at one of the residents called "Isabelle."

Isabelle sat across from me with a pot of string beans in her lap. She broke each bean and watched the television. Amelia then told her my name and said, "Maybe Marian will come back and read to you...wouldn't you like that, Isabelle?" Isabelle looked at me **hard** and finally nodded her head in affirmation that she'd approve of my return to the halfway house to read to her and with that we got up and left.

About a week later I walked with some friends from the dorm to the nearby Seven/Eleven store. The campus dining house was closed on Sundays so we were out shopping for frozen burritos and Top Ramen when I noticed Isabelle walking ahead of us. There she was in her thrift store 1960s dress, tattered blue sweater, knee-high nylons that didn't meet up with her dress and rubber soled tied shoes. She walked ahead of us and my friends ignored her as if they hadn't even seen her or as if she wasn't there. A part of me wanted to go up to her and say, "Hey, Isabelle, remember me? Marian from last week..." Instead I kept quiet and watched Isabelle walk ahead of us to the Seven/Eleven. I watched like a little bird scrutinize from a tree and as we bought our frozen burritos and Isabelle bought a bottle of Tequila wrapped in a small brown sack to drink on her way back to the halfway house.

Isabelle changed me in many ways. I became interested in working with children at risk for instance because of her. I wanted to do something to help people so that they no longer nurtured themselves through the Tequila bottle. In her way, Isabelle elicited a transition to adulthood for me.

Years later, I've looked back at what has happened in life; college, jobs, friends, lovers, children, pets, homes. We go through our lives and like Isabelle we may never be aware of who we leave our marks on. We do what we can for better and for worse and we hope that someone may hold a place in their hearts for us as we do for them. This is life and in it nothing stays the same. Life is transitory. It is movement, fluid with a flow that only stops for moments in time with winks of love and then it changes again. It is a blessing regardless.

There are times in life that feel extremely hard especially presently with the economy as it is. However, I've chosen to view this as instrumental to the spiritual growth of humanity. For instance, many people are unemployed and as hard as this is financially and emotionally I hold that there must be *spiritual* reasons for it. Consider the possibility that perhaps in a time that has been faster moving than in previous decades with technology, higher ambition, desire for money, prestige, etc., there maybe a need to slow down and take life in like I did on that walk when I was eight. I've been taught spiritually that there are reasons for everything and that everything happens for the best. We may not see this especially while it is occurring in our lives due to emotionality. It's hard, for instance, to see the good in struggling to find a job presently, but I do think that there is spiritual growth in this process. It's yet another of life's transitions and we may not be aware of the purpose that it serves until later. For example, I had no idea when I saw Isabelle at that Seven/Eleven that she would play a determinate role in my life, but she did.

In our modern times we want to have the best cars, computers, clothes with labels, etc. We want it all and we've been told that we can have it all, but what price does all of this come with? It may be higher than what is seen on the physical price tag.

I have often felt for the children of our world because so many are dropped off at schools early in the mornings and then not picked until late in the evenings five days a week. Some of these children also stay at the schools during holidays and over vacation periods essentially never having a break from their school lives. These children don't get to walk through the muddy pussy willows by themselves like I did. They live lives that are often rushed rather than nurtured.

These children lead very different lives than what I did as a child. My grandmother lived with us when I was growing up. It was sweet because someone was always at home which elicited a feeling of security for my brothers and I. I didn't have to spend my afternoons in daycares or go to school ill like so many of the children who I have taught do regularly. I don't blame the parents of these children. They have to do what they have to do, but there may come a time when they need to stop and reevaluate the priorities that they hold for themselves and for their children.

I'm at a time in my own life where I am reevaluating what has taken place and where I want to go next. This is a transitional stage. It's not easy, but it is important because it is vital to recognize the changes that we've made and what we would like still to accomplish. It is also critical to come to terms with the knowledge that what we want to execute may be unlike what we thought that we wanted ten or even five years ago. Life changes and so do we. This may be a time in history where we as spiritual people are called on to slow down and to give of ourselves differently than in the past. This may be a time where we are meant to use what we've been taught spiritually for the advancement of humanity. This isn't as easy as it sounds because it takes a profound amount of internal energy that needs to be renewed as quickly as it is used. It is a time therefore that we need to take care of ourselves physically, emotionally and spiritually so that we can help to heal this world.

As challenging as this time in history is it is also an amazingly powerful one where increasingly people are awakening to the spirit within.

I've seen, however, how this time in history is eliciting conflict with spirituality. A few weeks ago, an old friend from high school told me that she didn't want anything more to do with me because I didn't follow the same religion that she did. Somehow, my sense of the spirit frightened her which was the last thing that I had hoped for. I loved her and sincerely wanted for us to be life long friends, but that wasn't meant to be. At any rate, I think that friendships like anything else in life have their own karma and when that karma is extinguished the relationship ends.

Still, as a spiritual person my desire is never to frighten someone with what I believe in and because of this I tend to go easy with my friends with personal beliefs. For instance, I don't often tell them right off the bat that I have an East Indian spiritual teacher because this may scare them. I may not comprehend why they are frightened by this initially because in my mind my spiritual path is beautiful, but I also know how it is to feel pushed into something even when our friends are simply revealing to us their lives. For instance, when I was a teenager the friend who recently unfriended me took me to a "Born Again Christian Revival." This was her religion and it was completely unlike anything that I as a then little Catholic girl had yet to experience. These people spoke in "Tongues," waved their arms around in the air and claimed that their diseases had been healed by a single touch from the pastor. This was far from what I was used to in the Catholic Church where for the most part we sang in Latin, stood on command and kneeled when told to. The Catholic masses that I attended seemed much more "proper" than did this "Revival" which scared me because it was unlike what I was accustomed to. I didn't know what to think, but wanted nothing to do with what I was watching. Sometimes we have to go slowly with our friends so that there is understanding, grace and a willingness to see the good in what we have to offer. This sharing of ourselves is another of life's transitions that we can put forward with love though never push onto other people.

A few weeks ago, I got into a discussion with another friend who displayed fear of Muslim people. This fear is a hangover from 9/11. My friend displayed what appeared to be an obsession with her belittlement of the Muslim religion. While talking with her I attempted to persuade her that we can't begrudge an entire group of people because of some who come across as fanatics. My friend, however, was unable to hear this because her fear was deeply ingrained. She is unable to open her heart to see that there may be good in this particular religion because of what she saw with the terrorist groups. Often what we don't understand frightens us. I certainly saw this with myself and the "Revival" group. I see this in many people today and I think that it goes beyond religion or lack of.

Fear is what under roots our worst tendencies. It closes our hearts and our minds to other people and it makes it impossible for us to extend ourselves.

Unfortunately, we've also seen this with the recent "Occupy" group which started out with the most noble intentions though has left many killed.

These can be scary times, and yet, there is a spiritual pull that is profound. It is a calling for greatness despite fear. Courage after all is not the lack of fear. It is the ability instead to have faith despite one's fear. In today's world we are called on to have the kind of courage where we move through the mountains of destain and make a difference with the hearts and minds of the spiritual communities.

This energy is powerful because it permeates into the world and it heals. We need this today more than ever.

Life carries with it many transitions whether we see them as positive or not and they continue regardless. We grow up from childhood to teens and become young adults who strive for something that we may still be unsure of. We reach a state when in our adult years where we feel confidence. We may still be young, but we hold more certainty than we once did, yet, life changes again. We may lose our jobs, relationships, parents, etc., and we are thrown into life's harbor of pain, yet, somehow we get through it and we grow yet again. This is one of those times in history where we are propelled into a mysterious and sometimes scary cycle of growth. This can test our courage and spiritual bones though hopefully make us stronger.

Consider the time in history's past when our grandparents lived through the Depression Era. Somehow, they did whatever they could to get by. My grandmother took in tenants becoming a landlady in New York City. She got down on her hands and knees scrubbing the floors to take care of whatever she could. She raised her two children and her nephew while she also took care of her mother and her ill aunt. She was strong. I know that we have the internal strength of our ancestors. This is the gift that they handed to us to help us to get through difficult times. I have my grandmother's eyes and her fortitude.

In this time of great transition I urge you to strive toward the heart.

Rituals

When I was a little girl I loved to look at pictures of places that I had never been physically to though had a knowingness that somehow I had been there before. I'd fantasize about how I lived, what I looked like and of the clothes that I wore when I was in these places. This felt very real to me and even as an adult I have found myself drawn to certain pictures especially of women who I felt connected to. Some of these photos currently hang in my living room and ironically, people have often asked me if I had indeed posed for some of these photos myself!

Children have this knowingness of their past lives. The recognition may not be concrete, and yet, it is there as an avenue to what is within them.

I think that this may be why many of us are drawn to symbols of past cultures. For instance, I can't go into a church where there are large pieces of stained glass windows with gorgeous scenes on them without being in awe. I may not have the religious connection that these images draw us to, yet, I am somehow connected on a deep level when I stand in front of them. Cobble stone roads have the same effect on me as they also bring me back to a familiar place within me even though I may never have set foot there during this present life. These scenes elicit the memories of whole other lives that I know that I have lived during other times than the one that I am currently experiencing as my "reality."

Rituals also can elicit past memories as they bring us deeper within us to that place of recognition. Have you ever noticed how you are drawn to a specific tradition whether this was followed within your family or not? There is something about that particular ritual that pulls at your heart and makes you want it as part of your life.

When I was teaching I often did "Tea parties" with the children. With a lovely ceramic tea set and herbal teas or sometimes just juice I made this a very ritualistic time for the children on a daily basis. Every day at a certain time the children knew that we did what we called, "Tea time" and they loved and looked forward to it. Often the children helped me to prepare for the "Tea time." They walked with me into the kitchen, got out the tea or juice and watched as I heated it up and then walked again with me back to the classroom where we then sat in a circle to begin the ceremony as it truly was ceremonial. Always before we began we sat in silence just to observe the quiet and to go inside ourselves. This set the scene for the "Tea Time." I made eye contact with each child then and would ask the children what we were going to do and how we'd use our senses while drinking the tea. They'd then respond by saying that they'd use their eyes to *see* it, mouths to *taste* it, noses to *smell* the tea's scent and so on. We'd describe the tea and how it elicited our senses. After we said these various things I slowly and quietly poured each child a cup of tea. When this was completed we'd put our hands together and bow our heads to honor the spirit within all of us before finally drinking the tea. I laughed inwardly as some of the children would say, "Ahhhh" after they finished drinking their tea and placed their cups before them with delight.

This was a relatively quiet ritual which was done with toddlers. Can you imagine a group of two year old children sitting calmly in a circle to talk about their senses and to drink tea? They did this and loved it because it was our daily ritual which brought them into that quiet, still place within them where they connected to their own sense of spirit.

We've often been told that "silence is golden." Silence offers us an opportunity to touch upon the soul's wisdom because it takes us away from the chatter of the world and brings us inward to our Selves. It is important to offer this to our children at various times during the days especially with the consideration of how busy our lives have become whether at home, school or work. The reality is that these are different times than those when I was a child and could venture into the woods behind our home safely to contemplate and be one with the trees. Children need this time as do we adults to replenish the spirit. We need to make this part of our daily lives and rituals offer this as a way to go inward.

In a world where we are taught when very young to stand up for ourselves, fight the good fight and to make deals to acquire it is vital in our lives to take the time to honor the quiet that is there. In this sometimes chaotic world we need to make time for ourselves in this way. We have to carve it out and instill it as habitual.

I've seen that often times children and some adults like to fill up space with chatter and this happens more than likely because they feel that this is the way that they can get needed attention. However, this kind of attention takes them away from their own internal guide so when I've noticed them doing this I will try to bring them back to that place of calm. How?

There are many things that I did which helped the children to go inward. One such method was used on sunny days in which I brought out a large mat to a yard and laid down (if there was grass, I'd simply lay there without the mat). I rarely asked the children to join me, but inevitably they followed suit by laying down next to me. When they did this I asked them what they saw around them in a calm and quiet voice as if just to take it all in. We'd look at the clouds and notice the birds. We'd listen to the songs that these birds sang and take in the scents from the leaves, flowers or the recent rains. Often this didn't last for very long times, however, the children consistently would return to this spot after they ran around. Sometimes they would ask me to join them and other times they'd lay there by themselves. It amazed me to watch and see how they gravitated to this ritual. It inspired me to see how the children yearned to have a way to reconnect to that sense of spirit during their active and noise filled days.

Rituals like this are easy to create. They don't take much preparation and can be spontaneously inspired. For instance, try sitting outside or in a room quietly without bringing attention to yourself and you will find that the children will gravitate to you. They want the calm. Use "Quiet minutes" or "Silent time" as a way to help the children to go inward. Take them for walks and point out what is seen in the environment and listen to what they tell you by simply watching what they gravitate to. You will learn a great deal about the children and about yourself when you do these things.

It is important for adults too to find some kind of ritual that resonates with the heart. This could involve life's simplicity such as noticing the clouds or it could be prayer, meditation, lighting candles at certain times during the day or dancing before dinner.

When I was a little girl my parents made it a ritual to turn on their favorite Frank Sinatra music and dance just before dinner. My brothers, my grandmother and I sat at the dinner table in the dinning room while my parents danced in the dimly lit living room. I watched in awe as they laughed together in this way. I felt their love then and now as an adult know that this ritual helped to keep them close even during challenging times. It was *their* ritual which they allowed me to watch so it in turn it became my ritual as well.

Ultimately, I've found that rituals help all of us to go inward and find our "happy" place within. They bring us back to those places that we know that we've been to even if we've never set foot there in this lifetime. They connect us to our higher selves and to those places within us where anything is possible.

Remembering Love Before Me

It was early morning as she sat near the fire place to work on her New York Times crossword puzzle as she had for most of her adult life when he banged on the wall to alert her that he was awake. She put the puzzle and pen (yes, she did these incredibly challenging puzzles in pen) down and went to make his coffee. She put his three teaspoons of sugar into the cup and walked gingerly into the bedroom where she sat on the bed to talk with her husband as they had done each morning for over forty years.

She could not say that theirs had been a "perfect" marriage. She had contemplated divorce a couple of times. The first time she almost left him when she was thirty-three after thirteen years of marriage. She even started to date other men, but had returned to him. She loved him although she knew of the devil that lived within him. She also knew of the angel in his heart so she stayed through his cheating and his lies. She stayed and made it work though sometimes her heart broke.

She was seventeen when she met him. She caught his attention inadvertently when at a New York City deli where she and her high school girl friends met to sneak cigarettes. He nick named her, "Miss Park Avenue" and two years later they were married.

He was a first generation American from Irish immigrants. His father died from pneumonia when he was only three years old leaving his young mother with three babies. She remarried and had two more children with her new husband leaving her first three with her mother's family. His grandmother who only spoke Gaelic was a strict Catholic and attended mass every day. She was a good woman with a good heart and a good work ethic. She raised her own eight children and then her grandchildren all while working as a housecleaner in this new country where she couldn't speak the language. He adored his grandmother who taught him values and he became a boxer so that he could financially support the family including that of his mother's.

However, "Miss Park Avenue" thought that his boxing career was "violent" so she talked him into a career as a New York City police officer. She may not have seen that this career was just as violent in a different way, but it allowed for him to support their family and created separation from that of his mother's.

Two strikes against her being that she wasn't Catholic and the discontinuation of financial support made a rocky relationship for mother and daughter in law. Their wedding was held in the rectory of the church because she wasn't Catholic though she promised to raise their children as Catholics and vowed to take classes in Catholicism. She tried though was far from a hypocrite and although she continued to support him and their children as Catholics she never adopted this faith as her own.

They didn't have a child for the first eight and a half years of marriage. They struggled with this fact and finally had their first son; a golden haired boy. They were a young couple with a child and a cocker spaniel named Peter living in Astoria, New York where everything appeared rosy. Life began to change, they moved to the city and she told him that she wanted out of the marriage. They were fighting and she didn't think that he loved her. He begged her to stay and told her that everything would be different. He asked her to "date" which culminated in another pregnancy so they stayed together.

He became a detective and moved the family to California where they bought a big ranch style house, an Irish setter and a built in swimming pool. They raised their last two children in this lifestyle of sunshine and rain drops.

She sat on the bed watching her husband of over forty years drink his sweet coffee and sighed. Had it been worth it to stay together now with four children and this big house in Southern California? She wasn't sure, and yet, told herself that this was *her* life. She told herself that it was all good in the end. She still loved him despite the challenges that they had endured. Ultimately, she had grown up with him and in growing up life throws curves that make you who you are. She couldn't regret her choices.

This is the story of my mother and my dad. They had me in their forties and died when I turned thirty. I know that their love story was one of upheaval, but in conclusion it gave to them a life that was full and I miss them.

Still when she was a child her life was just beginning. They called her Ethel Virginia and she was born in Michigan. Her's was a typical story of a girl born to parents who adored her along with an older brother who she looked up to. Life was good and then the Depression struck. Life changed.

Her father, a Yale graduate and an engineer lost his job. This was monumental. Her dad, Ben Stone was a proud man and now was also unable to financially care for his family. He sought work everywhere and landed a job across the country all the way in California and it wasn't the job of his dreams by any means. This engineer landed a job with the California Conservation Corps, but it was a job during the Depression when most were out of work. For Ben, this wasn't half bad because this meant that he could move his family away from his wife's birth family. This meant moving away from his mother in law, his wife's mentally ill sister and her little boy. It wasn't that he didn't care for them and it wasn't that he was heartless, but he felt imposed upon. He felt as if his wife belonged to them and not to him so the move was a Godsend in his opinion.

His wife, Ada had a whole other impression about the idea of moving to California. It wasn't that she was opposed to moving, but leaving her family behind was out of the question for Ada. As far as she was concerned this family included her aged mother, mentally ill sister and her sister's little boy. She was furious with Ben for even considering leaving them behind. The couple began to fight for the first time in the marriage. They fought and they both dug their heals in deeper and deeper. Life was not good by a long shot for anyone.

Ben took off to California and told Ada that when he got settled he'd send for his family to join him. Ada told him basically to go to hell. She was just as proud as he was and just as stubborn.

Ada moved her family to New York City and bought a brownstone. She took in "borders" so that she could keep her family together regardless that this family no longer included her husband.

Ethel Virginia left her dolls and her childhood behind in Detroit. She grew up in the city. At first, her best friend was a taxi cab driver who took on the role of father. He watched over her, gave her advice and made sure that she was safe. She made friends with girls in the neighborhood and grew up to be tall, slender and beautiful.

When Ethel turned seventeen she met Ed at a deli where she and her girl friends regularly hung out to sneak cigarettes. Ed took one look at her and introduced himself. He called her, "Miss Park Avenue" because he said that she was the classiest girl whom he had ever met. Ed was a few years older than Ethel and handsome. He was the eldest of five children and a boxer. After a couple of years of dating Ed asked Ethel to marry him. She agreed if he promised to leave boxing and Ed became a New York City police officer.

All was wonderful and romantic for the then nineteen year old Ethel but Ed was an Irish Catholic and she had not been raised with any kind of religion. She told him that she was a non practicing Protestant but truthfully she was as agnostic as they come. She tried to study Catholicism and promised Ed that she would raise their children as

Catholics. This became a conflict for Ethel. She tried, but never fully accepted or adopted the Catholic religion.

It was almost ten years before they had their first child after many tries and struggles. They had a boy and named him after Ed's best friend, Gerald Kelly. Gerald was a beautiful golden haired boy who everyone stopped to look at. They lived in a small apartment in Astoria, New York with Gerald and their cocker spaniel, Peter. Life was good though as life does it changed.

Ed got promoted and they moved to Manhattan where they lived in a two bedroom apartment. It was okay at first. Ed was rarely at home and Ethel suspected that he was seeing other women. They fought and she asked for a separation. She started to date other men and prepared herself to be a single mother, but Ada stepped in and persuaded her to give Ed another chance. They dated a few times and at last culminated a date by making love in the living room of her mother's home. Ethel was confused, but when she learned that she was pregnant again she and Ed resumed their marriage.

They had another boy, Robert and six years later a girl named Marian. They planned to stop there, but got pregnant again two years later with another boy called Brian.

The two bedroom apartment was crowded with four children and Ada who had had a heart attack so needed more help than she could have had if she lived alone. It was so crowded that there was little privacy for anyone so Ed and Ethel moved their family out of the city and into the suburbs where they bought a four bedroom house. In that little house they continued to raise their children until the youngest two turned eight and ten. Then, Ed was offered a position as a detective in Southern California. This was an opportunity for a new start for the whole family so they made the move across country.

Life is never what your fantasies tell you that it could be and even though sunny California was indeed warm and beautiful there were struggles within the marriage. Ethel now in her fifties questioned Ed and almost left him but stayed mostly out of fear.

They didn't find contentment until later in life when Ed retired and he and Ethel moved to the Central Coast of California. They lived there happily for the last ten years of their lives. This was probably the happiest years that they had ever spent together. They lived there until both Ed and Ethel died of cancers.

Ethel was my mother and my ritual is to honor her on her birthdays. I miss her. I wrote this for her on Mother's Day~

I held your hand even if I didn't need to and you guided me when you no longer had to. You wiped away my tears when I fell and made me laugh when I was teased. You sang for me and I didn't care if you were out of key because I was your only girl.

You chased after me when I ran in the rain. You pretended that you couldn't find me when I hid from you. You gave me spaces to roam and allowed me to fantasize that I could fly. You watched from a distance and if I got hurt, you assured me that if I tried again, I'd succeed. You told me not to give up because after all I was your only girl.

You brushed my long hair when it snarled and when I got a comb stuck in it you laughed. You braided it and sprayed it with Johnson's, "No More Tears." You smoothed it with your fingers when the tangles got too rough to brush and when it was time to cut it away you said that I still looked beautiful because I was your only girl.

I called you once a week and even if distraught, when I heard your voice I was encouraged because you refused to give up on me. I know that I worried you at times. We fought. We yelled. You even slapped my face once and it stung for days longer than it should have. We said things that never should have been said yet your door to my heart never closed because I was your only girl.

When you got sick you went into the hospital on my birthday. It was the only birthday that you had ever ignored. I hated you for a minute. I was selfish and disconcerting. Still, you told me that you loved me and dad more than anyone else because I was your only girl.

You passed on to that other world where you can see me from a distance and I cried for a whole year. I heard your voice all the time regardless. I remembered your wise words, your directions, your suspicions, your guidance and suddenly that faded. I lost track somehow of you and yet still...today I remember only your love. I remember **you**

Stories Shared With Me

This is a story that was told to me by a friend and I thought that it was beautiful enough to include in this book:

Twenty-five years ago, I was fifteen and Olivia-Mia took birth. Then, I gave her up. I chose her parents from pictures and essays. The woman who raised her was ten years older than I. This age difference is nothing presently, but then, those years were the deciding factor of who would be *my* child's *mother*.

Through the years I wrote letters to my daughter.

July 25, 1985

To My Sweet Olivia-Mia,

This is your birthday; the day that you have taken on as your own; today is the day that you came into this world. It is the day that you also left my womb to be held by another mother. Today *my* heart is broken, but I give you to her with all my love and hopes for you to have a good life.

Love, Your Mommy

July 25, 1988

Dear Olivia-Mia,

I am eighteen now. I graduated from high school last month and am about to go to college. I'm moving away from my parent's house for the first time to be with kids who will have no idea that I've given birth to a beautiful little girl. I think about you all the time. I wonder if they call you, "Mimi" as I would have. You are three now. I wonder if you are in preschool and if you like it. I miss you. I even miss the kicks in the middle of the night that reminded me that you were with me.

Love from your Momma

July 25, 1992

Dearest Mimi,

Today is your seventh birthday. I hope that you have big helium balloons that fly through the sky to show you that anything that you dream of can come true. I want that for you. I miss you, Sweetheart. Mommy just graduated from college. I have a BA in Advertising. I want to write, but someday, Mia more than anything else I want to see *you* again. I think about you all the time.

Love, Your Mom

July 25, 1997

Dear Olivia,

On my twelfth birthday my mother told me that I was a "woman" because I started my period. If you have cramps or *any* kind of pain, I wish that it was me who held your hand. Please don't rush growing up, Olivia, as I did. Take your time and be *with every* moment of your life.

Much love, Your Mom

July 25, 2000

Dear Oliva-Mia

Today you are the same age that I was when you were born. I was fifteen then and am thirty now. I'm married to a great guy who loves me. We want to have children, but he doesn't understand that fifteen years ago I *had* a child. He knows about you, but he doesn't *get* it. He doesn't realize how much you still mean to me even after all this time. I hope that you are a happy high school girl; maybe even a cheerleader or someone with many friends. I clung only to your dad which was a mistake. I grew up too fast. Don't do what I did, Olivia-Mia. Take your time.

July 25, 2003

Dear Olivia-Mia,

I have exciting news to tell you! Today I learned that I am pregnant. Olivia-Mia, you will soon have a little brother or sister! I'm happy, Olivia-Mia, and yet, tears are running down my face as I write this. You are now grown up and I haven't seen you since the day that you were born eighteen years ago. I missed out on brushing your hair and walking you to school. I wish that you were here with me, but somehow, I think that you *are* with me telling me about your plans for college.

I love you--your Mom

July 25, 2005

Dearest Olivia-Mia,

Life has been really hard over the past couple of years. My baby died. It was a boy and he died shortly after he was born. They said that there was something wrong with his heart and it just stopped. I've been depressed. My husband doesn't understand. He wants to try to have another baby, but I can only think about the two that I've given birth to. We fight a lot; he and I and I don't think that we're going to make it. I miss you.

Your Mom

July 25, 2008

Dear Olivia-Mia,

Today is your twenty-third birthday! I bought a cake to celebrate and I did something else too. I went down to the adoption agency to see if I can find you. My life feels incomplete without you, my daughter. I want you in my life. You are part of me and always have been. You are in my blood and in my soul. I pray that you will be open to meeting me and that you will not hate me for giving you up twenty-three years ago.

July 25, 2010

Dear Olivia-Mia,

You are twenty-five today and at last I get to hold you as *my* child. I love you so much, do you know that? I look at you and feel that we've never been separated. In another month I will attend your wedding. I am blown away by what time has done to both of us. I gave birth to you when I was a fifteen year old confused little girl and now I am forty; middle aged and happier than I've ever been. Today, you are an adult and about to begin a new life. I am grateful that finally you and I can share our lives. We will have many tomorrows together!

Much love, Your Mom

This too was shared with me from a time before my own:

She was waif-like at five feet two inches tall and childlike thin. Her thick blonde hair slid to the bottom of her ass. She entered into UCBerkeley appearing fourteen and yet was beguilingly beautiful.

The year was 1968; a world of turmoil when life itself was uproarious.

Unlike tiny Paige, I came from conservative parents in the Midwest. We lived in small town Illinois where the houses looked alike with little gardens, white picket fences and one dog in the yard. Mine was certainly no exception. I hated it and wanted out so when I got accepted to UCBerkeley I was more than thrilled. I was scared too, but couldn't wait to get there. I knew that my life would never be the same once I was there.

I had boxes and carts of clothes, books, albums and more to lug into the dorm, but when I arrived Paige was already unpacked and settled in. She seemed completely calm and when I asked if she needed help she pointed to one small suit case and said, "That's it!" It was tiny just like she was, but I knew immediately not to let appearances be the guide.

That night Paige and I had dinner at the dining commons. We talked about our backgrounds and our families. She lived in San Francisco, her father was a doctor and her mother taught classical piano. She knew of the great operas and talked about Nixon with disgust all in one sentence. She said that her boyfriend had fled to Canada to avoid the draft. She told me about a demonstration that was planned for the next day and urged me to attend it with her. How could I refuse?

There were maybe a hundred people when we arrived that morning at the Bell Tower. Paige waved at a man who walked over to us. He looked about twenty, his long stringy brown hair hung past his shoulders and he wore wire rimmed glasses. Paige immediately threw her arms around his shoulders in embrace. He kissed her lips and shoved pamphlets at me to hand out to the crowd. I felt a little lost at what to do, but Paige was completely in her element. She grabbed the pamphlets out of my hands and ran toward people calling out to them to get involved. She screamed, "War is not healthy for children and other living things."

She yelled quotes that I had seen on posters looking gloriously radiant. Who wouldn't want to follow her anywhere?

An hour later the crowd was enormous with long haired teenagers and people in their early twenties carrying signs and chanting to end the war. I got completely swooped up in the excitement as if the chant itself was some kind of drug or maybe it was the scent of the marijuana which was abundantly in the air. I breathed it in to affirm that I was no longer in the Midwest. I was no longer my "Daddy's little girl."

Someone pushed a microphone in my face and I realized that it was a Television news reporter complete with cameras as if I was someone important and had something to say. I muttered something about my "philosophy on life being more important than was war" when the same man who I had met with Paige pushed me aside to spew out obscenities about Nixon. I watched as if witnessing from a far away place and just then saw mounds of police officers coming our way with guns and gas bombs. Their amplified calls shouted at us to leave the premises. I looked around for Paige, but she was so tiny that there was no way that I could find her in that crowd. For the first time that day or even in my life I was terrified.

I would have left at that point if not for Paige. There was no way that I was going to leave her there. I roamed through the crowds pushing my way against bodies to find her, but didn't see anywhere. It was as if she had disappeared into thin air, but the police on the other hand were everywhere and suddenly one of them had grabbed my arm tugging at me and yelling that we had been warned to leave.

For the first time in my entire life I found myself in jail. I called my dad. He screamed, "What in the hell have you gotten into?" He threatened to come to Berkeley to escort me home where he said that I "belonged." Still, he bailed me out of jail.

When I got back to the dorm that night I found Paige in bed with that man with the pamphlets. She smiled at me disconcertingly.

I crawled into my own bed. I pulled the blankets over my head, pretended that I didn't hear them and prayed that they didn't hear me sob until I finally fell asleep.

That was my initiation into life at UCBerkeley.

After that day, I became more involved in the war against the war than even Paige had been and eventually made my way to Vietnam where I worked as a nurse. I saw many a young person die over there and I got to help save the lives of a few.

What Momma Taught Me

Twenty Things That My Mother Told Me That Are Actually True!

1. Eat only when you are hungry and stop just before you are full.
2. Don't take other people's word for gospel. Consider what they have to say and think it over before you believe it to be "true."
3. Don't wear your heart on your sleeve or people will take advantage of you. Be smart about who people are.
4. Get to know people before you decide to trust them.
5. Read something even if it is just a crossword puzzle every day and this will keep your mind sharper.
6. Live an active life, don't sit for too long or your ass (although my mother never used the word, "Ass!" LOL) will be telling.
7. Take care of your feet and they will take care of you for the rest of your life. If you wear shoes that are too tight, you will have feet problems always.
8. Don't work too physically hard because this is not good for the body and the pain will come up later in life.
9. Drink only in moderation especially in public because if you make a fool of yourself, people remember this.
10. Be able to support yourself financially and don't depend upon a man to take care of you. He may

leave you, you may not want to stay with him, and if the relationship is good, this will keep it positive.

11. Only tell people what you want for them to remember. If you tell too much, you may regret this later and won't be able to take it back once said.

12. Watch and observe before making decisions.

13. Family is important.

14. No one's family is The Brady Bunch and there will always be little issues between people.

15. Forgive your family members so they can forgive you.

16. Put things in their proper places and you won't struggle to find them later.

17. Be pleasant to the waiter, salesperson, etc., because life has a way of bringing people back together.

18. Take your time when you make decisions and don't allow others to rush you into anything.

19. A woman's hair is her crown so take care of it and mayonnaise makes a great hair conditioner.

20. Lies have a way of coming out so be truthful.

Twenty Things That I Would Tell My Daughter

1. Don't let fear get in your way of doing what you want to do.

2. Show your love to people and to yourself by being true to who you are.

3. Have an open and flexible heart.

4. Take care of your teeth; floss every day and rinse with that icky tasting amber colored Listerine.

5. Exercise a little every day.

6. Do what you enjoy doing at least a little each day.

7. Meditate every morning.

8. Don't hold onto anger because in the end it hurts you more than those who you are angry with.

9. Learn to love with detachment and don't take in other people's issues.

10. Everything in life is non-permanent so enjoy the present moment and if it is challenging, remember that it too will pass.

11. Take risks with your heart and with your talents because if you hold back, you will regret this later.

12. Don't expect for other people to do things as you would. It's okay if other people do things unlike how you do them--be flexible and open-minded to other people's ways of being.

13. Learn to live without expectations and disappointments will be fewer.

14. Trust your intuition because it will guide you.

15. Care about your friends but don't hold onto them. When the karma that you have with each person is exhausted the relationship will be done. Be okay with that. You can send the person blessings and love regardless.

16. Recycle and take care of the Earth for it upholds you.

17. Honor your dreams by writing them down. They hold messages of wisdom just for you.

18. Drive carefully.

19. Think before you speak and act. Pause first, breath and observe the energy around you before saying or doing anything.

20. Watch where your breath lies and listen to your heart rate because this indicates whether you are doing the right thing, in good company and more. It is your compass!

Childhood Educational Beginnings

If you have a child or have hopes for the children of this world (and you should), it is important to consider what we want for preschools because in today's world most children spend a huge amount of time in these places therefore are molded as societal people while growing and maturing while in schools.

Foremost, think about what kind of school would excite and interest you. What are your goals for the children of the world and what do you want to be presented to the children while they are in schools? Are there specific ethics that you'd like to be honored, as well as traditions and insights? Consider these because the children of our world learn and adapt to the environments that they are in while they are very young. This will influence the rest of their lives.

Some schools, for instance, celebrate only specific holidays while others make attempts to honor all of them and some choose to ignore them all. What do you want for the children of this world to be exposed to? Do you believe, for instance, that children must learn the pledge of the United States? Should prayer be completely eliminated in schools? Should children be exposed to various cultures and languages other than those that they are taught at home? How should children be disciplined and what social moral values should children be taught at school if any? Consider all of these things and more because they will eventually effect how our world is being taken of by these only young now people.

In the preschool culture teaching is fairly dominated by women and you may want to seek a male teacher. You might even consider hiring or finding a school that has both a man and a woman in the classroom. Take Tom and Lily, for instance. Lily is creative and nurturing, but when she calls out, "Clean up time" the children ignore her. Tom, on the other hand, commands attention with his lower voice.

However, many parents worry when it comes to having a man change diapers or even give discipline. If this is your school or is the school of your choice, be prepared to advocate for your male teacher because in today's world he may need your support.

If you are a parent or are opening up your own school, consider what you want from a teacher before you start the interview process. I say "interview process" because you will want to interview everyone involved in the school. Do your homework and don't look only at the school's owner or director. Check out the teachers because they will be with your children during most of your child's time at school. Do you want the teacher to have a specific amount of education and experience? Should this person be prolific in a particular philosophy say Developmentally Appropriate Practices or Montessori for instance? What qualities do you aspire for yourself and for your children? How will the teacher represent these qualities?

You can tell a great deal from a resume including years of experience and education as well as job longevity. Keep in mind, however, that preschool teachers tend to job hop more than other professionals do. This is because of the general pay and benefits in this occupation as well as a teacher's desire to learn. The teacher who has stayed in one place for at least a year shows a degree of commitment which is important because children require consistency. Although, when hiring or checking out a teacher you should keep in mind that the teacher who has worked with various populations and modes of teaching also brings a wealth of experience to your school and her growth has not been stagnant. You should appreciate what she can bring to the table with past experiences that may include an assortment of traditions, styles and methods of teaching.

During the interview remember what this job entails. The teacher needs to be able to do physical work that is demanding as well as emotionally draining. What are some of the subtle signs to look for that may indicate that she or he can handle this job? Is the applicant dressed to the nines wearing four inch heels, long finger nails and too much perfume? She might be great in another line of work, but probably is not suited for a preschool.

You've got your questions ready, you've researched the resumes and in essence you've now done your homework. It's now time for you to sit down with the applicants and for them to show if they too have done their homework. Ask what the teacher believes that a school should do for a child. Get to know what the teacher finds important and what this person who will spend a great deal of time with your little one will honor. This will tell you how interested the person is as well as how motivated they are to do the little extras that are always required in preschools.

Be prepared to ask scenario questions because these will give you the opportunity to see how well the teacher can handle actual events that take place in a preschool daily. For example, "It's lesson time and Johnny is running around. What do you do?" The teacher's answer reveals her style. She may redirect Johnny with reminders or suggestion of lessons. She may ask him what he is doing and why. Ask yourself what you are seeking in a teacher because this scenario indicates how the teacher will handle the classroom environment.

Remember to ask about how the teacher handles parents. Does the applicant have experience with parents? Does this person have the finesse to handle the parent who might get in his or her face? Is she gracious, calm, gentle, sweet though steadfast and professional? Is the teacher "too friendly?" A good teacher is friendly and open, though also has boundaries with parents to maintain professionalism.

The teacher is responsible for the classroom which can get hairy fast. Is she organized, easy going and on top of things? It's about balance. You want to seek the teacher who is able to maintain a classroom that is calm, fluid and fun at the same time. Does the teacher think that limits are important? A well balanced teacher knows that limits make a child feel safer. This teacher will neither set too many limits or too few creating balance for the calm and fluid classroom.

Good luck because the reality is that you can have the most beautiful and well equipped school, but it's the teacher that is the most important ingredient for any well run classroom. What do you want for the teachers who help to raise the children of this world? Think about this because ultimately these people influence the molding of our world which starts with the children.

Honor your schools as they are currently developing tomorrow's society.

Play!

The sun beat against her browned skinned back as she ran into the ocean thrusting her body against the break of the waves. Her laughter chimed with the breeze as she dove into the crash and her body spun with pure audacity. She was a child of the ocean and on another day in late September when the leaves turned auburn she gathered them into a huge pile and jumped. Kicking them they scattered wildly as she danced to her own autumn child's tune of *play*.

Don't you remember the days when you made awkward snowmen with coal eyes and your father's old scarf or when you threw snowballs at your brothers and laughed when one hit your neighbor by surprise? Maybe those days feel too long ago to recall, but deep in your memory bank they thrive and you *still* **play**.

Children naturally and curiously take life on with enthusiasm. Their eyes grow large and light up when something strikes them as "fun." Nothing is "too silly" and life is easily adventurous. For me, these escapades will always be in my mind's catalogue of great times.

For instance, I remember walking with my brother through the shells of houses that were being built near where we lived when I was about eight. We were warned not to go there. We were told that there might be nails and other "dangerous" things, but wandered into these houses regardless. We walked through the "living rooms" and declared which room would be *our* bedrooms. These were brand new homes that were not completed, but we told "ghost" stories about the "old woman" who roamed the halls carrying a stick. We created scenes for these homes that had yet to be lived in for the sake of entertainment because it was fun and in our imaginations *anything* was possible. The smell of the wood, the imposing thought that we were doing what we told not to do and our resourceful innovations elicited a simple adventure that I will never forget.

We all grow up quickly. We forget about those times when we ran through the tall grass or slid down the hill only to land in the mud. We forget about how we heartily laughed while riding our bikes down the steepest slopes even when these times left us with bloody knees. Time goes by and we lose track of those playful days as we instead merge ourselves into the world of the serious "grown ups." We get lost in the traps of making money, developing ambition and creating names for ourselves. We gain what we *think* are our identities, and in the process, we relinquish the knowledge of who we really are.

Some say that life is meant to be taken **very** *seriously*. After all, they further add that we "only have one life to live." I don't believe in this theory. Instead, I know that we have many lives to learn, grow and evolve and that laughter is one of the best ways to metamorphose. It changes and improves us regardless because it brings us back to our hearts.

When we recognize the importance of laughter we know that play shouldn't be cast aside because we've added a few years onto our annual belts. I've often seen that the elderly are the least egotistical. Their golden hair may now sparkle with a bit of silver, and yet, they know the importance of 'silly.' When you let go of the ego's hold you realize that your imagination is still just as vibrant as it was when you were seven and when you tap into this you enjoy the simple fun of having a playful spirit which costs nothing. Further, when you let go of your egoistic need to be right, seen as important and as a poker faced "adult" you find that there is magic in play. The charm of this enjoyment takes you back to the child's sense of freedom and lets you reconnect with your divinity.

Renowned Child Developmentalist Jean Piaget said that children learn best when they play. By the means of play the child comes to assimilate his environment through his senses and uses play to discover his world. He accommodates differences, classifies objects and learns inclusion, conservation and to discriminate one from another all through the adventures of play. He learns social skills and comes to learn how he is part of the world when he plays. Play, therefore is the child's work and is important as this is how the child learns while he discovers the world and who he is in relationship to the world that he lives in.

Play may be the child's work, but who said that the adult's job should not *include* play or be fun? Who said that the adult must relinquish the word "silly" when "mature?"

Perhaps the way that we go about our sense of play as adults may be dissimilar to that of the child's, and yet, it is in this adventure of letting go that we lose what weighs us down and helps us to gain our sense of hope again. The reality is that we may no longer find merry go rounds as thrilling as we did when we were five, however, we can't help but still see the beauty in the painted horses. Some people may feel that they may need a more "sophisticated" form of play for enchantment to entice them into enthusiasm. For instance, these people may require expensive ski trips while others unpretentiously play in the snow and have a great time, but ultimately both experiences will lighten the load of life. Regardless of how you choose to spend your "play" time this is a vital part of life. So, whether you need the clang of the coins and lights of Las Vegas for a weekend of fun or are one who can merely sit by a pool with a good book and a pretty tropical drink it doesn't matter as long as you spend time in play because this will bring you back to your true nature and will improve your live immensely.

Get out from under the office lights and away from the computer desk for some silly time occasionally and you will live a fuller life. You can choose to spend money on expensive trips, however, you can also simply go for car drives, take long walks, run, swim, etc, to have fun. The only thing that is required of you is for you to let go of your sense of tightness and allow yourself to *play*.

Take one sunny Sunday morning and turn on your stereo as loudly as you want to dance in your living room in your underwear without any concerns about how you appear. You will find that the more that you allow yourself to be silly the closer that you will come to your highest Self.

This is true because when you do these things you will find that you will turn your attention away from life's heaviness and become lighter literally. It will be as if the sun was lit directly from within you because you will discover that the greatness of life comes with *ease*. You will also begin to discover that play brings out the best in everyone.

I remember one family Thanksgiving that was becoming increasingly stressful. There was an abundance of food; a real cornucopia to be had, and yet, no one was having a good time. The table was beautifully set and then someone made a remark that this gorgeous work of art table had **better** not be *messed* up. We sat down not with eagerness, but with apprehension that we might get yelled at for doing *something* "wrong." We ate the food and complimented each other's contributions to the meal and then complained about the dishes that were now piled high to be washed as we sat feeling stuffed and uncomfortable. One by one we got up and carried our dish to the sink and a few of us started to wash the dishes in a morose kind of silence. We continued in this fashion of not wanting to upset the already upset when somebody splashed soapy water onto someone else. Suspicious glances were cast around the room and then someone else threw more soap suds at another *innocent* dish washer. Suddenly, we all burst into laughter. We were soaking wet, but the tension was broken and we were again a family who loved and cared for each other.

Play. It will do you good!

Never Alone

Holidays and birthdays elicit reflection. This reflection can be anticipated, but sometimes it is blindly thrust upon us cruelly with remorse. Still, life whether we approve of it or not continues to move ahead.

Time is healing and time can be a monster that leads us to old age where our bodies wither like snow dripped leaves on lifeless trees.

My heart beats rapidly as if out of control and I am hot despite cold temperatures. I open windows just to breath. In shock I wonder what happened to the life that I planned out for myself at twenty? Where did my babies go and that wonderful man who danced with me at the various parties that we "were" to attend--once upon a time?

Where did "we" go? Did "we" evaporate as "I" became a woman who ventured into a life cast for me with laughter and hell-bent sorrows? Where did "I" go and when did I vastly change?

The little girl inside me reached out with her small hands to be guided as she stepped forward into the street while cars whizzed by. She trusted me with her green eyes to keep her safe in the world that she was yet to advance into.

I look at her now as if she is just a mirage and maybe she is a figment of my imagination, but, there she is staring at me with bewilderment as the life that she sees ahead is not what she hopes for. This life is not what she created in story books. It is not like those that she colored in with her crayons of rainbows. It lacks the fancy dresses and lip glossed kisses, but, somehow it is the life which "I" chose.

How did that happen?

This life that has both scared and challenged me has been the one that I alone have been responsible for. No one could have created it better than I did, right? Yet, truly I was not completely the creator for this would be egotistical, yes? I am after all not the "doer" for the one who does everything resides within my heart and connects me to my source of the divine. This is the God that is within all of us and manifests as One group of humanity.

My life has been one of sharing with hands held and tears wiped by those who loved me and those who have been there with me in the worst of it as well as during the loudest, most forceful times of laughter. I was alone during times when I anticipated caresses. I was by myself though never abandoned. I felt small only when my fear allowed this to play out. I was never as "alone" or as small in reality as that of my mind's harboring. God was always with me.

I heard Oprah once say that as a child she knew that she was "meant for greatness." I never thought of myself as "great" and see nothing that I've done in this life as tremendous, and yet, know that there is potential within all of us. We all have the will of divinity that makes everything possible. It is only the mind that elicits the veil that creates life's most obscure which leaves us in the ego's darkened avenues of fear and disdain.

Birthdays and holidays draw us into reflection and sometimes this creates a force that is anew. It is fresh and awaits for us to draw upon it like a blank canvas for only each one of us to paint in any way that we want for it to look. It is there for me as "I" see it to detail my life with just the right strokes and colors of "my" choosing.

We'll see next year what I do with this new canvas and if this develops as I see it presently, however, in this moment, it is all that I have and it is: freedom.

How about you? How do you see the life that you have created so far? Will you take it with new eyes to draw adventures that inspire you and maybe even frighten you because this is not what you imagined in your past? Or will you take the canvas that you've created with your life as it is and build upon it for more of the same? Either way, it's yours to do as you want to do with your most perfected strokes and colors.

It is about freedom.

"*Everything's* dead. *Nothing's* alive and it's *cold*. I **hate** this time of the year!" So said my best friend when I was seven, but... It was my birthday, and it was two weeks from Christmas, and it was the first snow fall of the year.

I wore holly in my hair that year and a corsage that my brother made with little pieces of Wrigley's pink bubble gum. I danced in the snow with my arms stretched outward to catch every little snow flake because it was my birthday and it was the first snow fall of the year.

My mother made me Boston cream pie because that was my favorite. I loved the pudding in the center and the velvety chocolate on top, but the best dessert by far was the snow that my brothers and I collected to pour maple syrup onto. This was the best dessert because it was my birthday and because it was the first snow fall of the year.

My father helped us to make a snow man. It was a ton of work and took almost all day. It was taller than I was and when we finished my father let us use one of his scarves to wrap around the snowman's neck. There he stood with coal in his eyes and a carrot for a nose looking mighty pretty to my eyes because it was our snow man on my birthday and it was the first snow fall of the year.

My dad was tired by the end of the day and it was almost dusk, but I begged him to take us to "Lederle's" hill where we could go sledding. We carried our long toboggan to the hill along with pillows because if I fell out of the toboggan as I often did down that steep hill, I'd be protected with the softness of the pillows. My father thought in those terms for my safety and for my comfort. I drug the pillows literally to the hill as they were almost bigger than I was while dad carried the toboggan on my seventh birthday and during the first snow fall of the year.

We were wet and cold by the time that we had at last finished on that hill. My dad wanted to go home, but my brother and I pleaded with him to ice skate. We were still little and wobbly on our skates so we skated on the pond near the hill wearing our boots. I could have stayed out all night. I didn't care that it was December and that I was wet and cold. It was my birthday and it was the first snow of the year.

When we finally went home my mother said that she had made a special birthday dinner, but she refused to serve it before I took a hot bath. She smiled and told me that I could use my first birthday present--bubbles for the bath. They smelled sweet and felt soft against my skin as I sat in the foggy tub lingering with the memory of the first snow fall of the year.

Dressed in flannel pajamas I sat at the dinner table with my family. I wanted to race through dinner just to get to that cake. It was my favorite after all, but my mother made me slow down to taste the meal that she had prepared for my birthday and for the first snow fall of the year.

I snuggled under a brand new quilt that night while visions of snow falling from the sky soothed me to sleep. The cascades of the whiter than white flakes took me to dreams of my seventh birthday and of the first snow fall of the year.

It's been many years since then and I now live in a place where it doesn't snow on my birthdays. Still, however, I will always hold in my heart the times that I caught those snow flakes with my then small hands. I remember when it was my seventh birthday and the first snow fall of the year.

When she was four years old her parents decided that she would be an "only child." She became a creative child who made toys out of boxes. She became an inventive child who found ways to build and a studious child who taught herself things. She was also imaginative. She listened to the sounds of the spirits around her. She was never bored and she never felt alone.

When my friend was in elementary school she was not the child who chased after others. She did her own thing. When in high school she didn't fit in with the "cliques" and she wasn't one of the "popular girls." This didn't bother her.

In her senior year she fell in love for the first time. Her boyfriend took her to dinners and movies. They talked on the telephone for hours and finally they made love, however, one day after many months of dating he said, "I'm not ready to get serious" and he ended the relationship.

In college she moved out of her parent's home and into her own apartment which she shared with another young woman who she became close friends with. Together she and her roommate sat up until wee hours of the mornings talking about everything and anything. They shared coffee and wine, clothes, jewelry, boyfriends, thoughts, ideas, hope. They shared life until one day her friend announced that she would soon transfer to an out of state college and move away.

When she graduated from college she began her career as an advertising copywriter and fell in love for the second time. Unlike her previous relationship this was serious and she got married. Together she and her new husband bought a house and a year later had a baby boy. They worked long hours and spent their weekends "catching up." They lived this fast paced life for twenty years until she received a call from the nearby hospital while at work. Her husband had had a massive heart attack and was dead at forty-two.

Her son married young and she became a grandmother. She spent her weekends babysitting and doting on her grandchildren. They were an extension of the life that she had known with her husband until her daughter in law told her that she "needed space." A month later her son called and told her that they were planning on moving out of state.

She became friendly with one of the women whom she worked with. This friend invited her to a spiritual center where she learned to do yoga and meditate. She was introduced to a spiritual master and received what was called; "Shaktipat" which she was told was the awakening of her divine energy. Afterward, she sat in a chair with closed eyes and felt this energy rise from her tail bone and upward through her spine. She felt it cascade around her. She felt as if she was spinning within the energy, moving around and around and upward within her own body! She had never felt anything like this. The energy continued to pulsate through her body spinning her and she sensed that it was about to unleash itself through the top of her head. It was more powerful than anything that she had ever known and suddenly she wasn't sure that she could survive it. She opened her eyes and took several deep breaths. Her Kundalini had been awakened and she knew that God had touched her.

Her life was changed completely.

From that day forward she knew that no matter who came into her life or who left her life she would **never** be alone.

God was within her as her. This realization had made her aware that she had all the power within to manifest a life of the divine. She knew that this was her destiny and she smiled. She knew love because she knew herself.

She began to experience angels who visited her. She had dreams that came true and she was spoken to by prophets. She saw energy around other people and she saw spirits. She moved in the realms of the highest lights. She knew that anything was now possible!

When you know your most divine self you are **never** alone.

Conclusion

Before we came into the world we made an agreement with God about what we wanted to learn this time around and we trusted in the process. We came into this world with open minds and wide hearts that what we chose to be done in our lives would be accomplished. We also made agreements who would be in our lives to clean karma up with.

We came into this world with a huge amount of potential for expansion as spiritual beings. We had everything that we needed within us which was given to us directly from God to execute, create and heal the world with. We had a tremendous mission ahead of us and we took this on willingly and with the enthusiasm of the knowledge that we had God's blessings for this journey. We took this on fearlessly to fulfill this mission called our lives.

Then, however, we came into the world as tiny manifestations of life within small human being bodies, yet, our spirits had infinite amounts of knowledge that we could use within any moment to help and guide us along the way. This was ours to tap into and it was completely assessable to us for whenever we wanted or needed it. The only vulnerability that we had was the fact that we came in the small packages which we arrived in physically because the spirit within was magnificent and broader than daylight itself. This spirit held no limitations for us as our lives were meant to be lived with freedom and for greatness.

Still, as these tiny beings we were planted into the arms of those whom we had great karma with. Our mothers took us to their breasts to feed us, nurture us and educate us in the ways of the world. She spoon fed us what she thought that we needed so that we could stay strong and to get ahead. She did the best that she could with the help of someone else who we also had karma with. Our fathers took us outside to rough us up so that we could take on what would later be thrown at us by the world. He wanted for us to catch that ball of courage and we did. We listened to our elders' words with fevered eagerness to learn and we did the best that we could because ultimately we only wanted to please though who loved us the most.

When we got a little bigger we went into the world for the first time. This may have happened in Kindergarten or preschool. It could have been even sooner than that as many of us were plopped on into the arms of these often not so gentle worldly beings while we were still infants. Seemingly strangers took us out of the warm arms of our parents to further mold and guide us into the ways of the world. We are lucky if they were kind, open minded and wise. We were fortunate if these strangers saw the good in us as many of these people treated us like herds to be thrusted into groups and as a result often we lost ourselves then.

We may have complained to our parents but they were too busy to hear our cries. The reality was that they were trying only to survive as best that they could and they told us then to buck it up for this is just how the world is. The world as we knew it then became unfriendly, uncaring and even scary. It certainly was not *welcoming* of who we were and who we still are. With this lack of graciousness we hid who we are even from ourselves and we forgot all that we knew when we came to this plane of life. We let go of our intuitions and we surrendered our hearts to the ambitions that are of the world. We became colder and harder because we felt that this was what we had to do just to survive in this world. We then lived in our egos instead of our hearts.

This is the cycle that we came to know and it is what we have transferred to our children so that we could teach them how to get by in this often frightening world. We ignored who are our children really are as we also ignored this within ourselves. We have robbed the children of their greatness as our parents and teachers did to us. We made them smaller instead of more magnificent mostly due to our fears of what we thought that the world was, and in turn, we created a scarier world for ourselves and for the children.

Consider that if we adults began to teach our children to honor who they are, their intuition and their hearts, we invite them to use the gift of the knowledge that they came here with. This supreme information is within all of us when we learn to acknowledge and tap into it. Know too that when we are able to manifest this within ourselves we can give our children a sense of freedom to have what they truly deserve which is why they are here on this planet today. They will, in turn, create a world of love that is higher, happier and more potent than anything that we have yet to know. There will be no boundaries that can hold the potential of their greatness back and we can give this to them **now** simply by honoring who they are.

It is time now to make needed changes in the world where we live for ourselves and for the children who will take this world on as their own one day. This is a powerful time of transformation that will heal and elevate life to higher dimensions where we can once again communicate telepathically, know everything through intuition and have heart bonds with each other. We can create a world that is higher than the one that we know as worry based with incredible potentials for amazing miracles. The possibilities are within us all when we overcome our fears and trust in our divinity.

Trust in the process of you and you will come to know who you are. Have faith in the inner guide that is your own holy nature and you will be able to manifest anything that you want for your life as well as heal the world as we know it today.

We can do this if we believe in the hearts of Oneness.

Poems of Love

The Touch Of The Butterfly~

Gentle sapphire waves
came into my life
whirling me
into rapture
on hands and knees
to behold
your almond shaped eyes
that embraced the Universe
with one glance.

Those eyes~

gentle me.

I see them when I'm not looking.
I feel them in my dreams in the middle of the
darkened nights.
I hear them
in *your* thoughts
and my entire body trembles stirring
from the diamonds that light up the ebony skies.

Perceive me as a ghost of girl
if you will think of me at all, but know
that I am in awe of your radiance.

There is no one alive like you.

Brilliant intuits have no idea of your love's depths.
They have no clue of what you bestow
on someone as humble
and small as me.

I wait now cross legged
and close my eyes to visualize
the luminance of my beloved
as gentle winds take me into the dance
of the rage within and I laugh
as the tears flow
moistening my sensitive heart.

Somehow, despite it all I feel the flutter
that touches my cheek as if a tickle
and open my eyes to see the beautiful
and graceful butterfly dancing in the light
with ebony wings highlighted by electric blue
and I know that it's you.

Dragonflies For Sofia~

Dragonflies
and pretty little birds
bumble bees
and butterflies

fluttery little things
singing with their wings
dancing in the clouds
giving hope
for yet another day
filled by love's
remembrance

of dragonflies
and pretty little birds,
bumble bees
and butterflies

dancing in the clouds
singing with their wings
fluttery little friends
making space for Sofia
up above the world
in a sky of blueberry cream…

dragonflies
and pretty little birds
bumble bees
and butterflies

singing with their wings
and dancing
in the clouds…

Come To Me~

You come to me
whispering words

I need to hear
as you talk to me
in my sleep.
You find me where
I want to go
cause in your eyes
I'm never lost.

Come to me
and sing your songs.
Make me yearn deep within~
you know exactly what I need
because you're there
for me
when nothing's right.

Come to me
in my dreams
and show me
where I'm complete.
Let me see
the maps to you.
You know exactly
what I need
when you
wrap your heart
around my soul.

You come to me
when others
leave me cold.
You let me see
the invisible

and tell me it is
still
possible.

You come to me
and make
this world's wrongs
transient.
You touch upon
the radiance
that
I never knew
inside of me.
You let me
see this
intervention
of goodness
in everyone.

You come to me
and unveil
discussions
of might
again and again.
You come to me
with your
shining heart.
You come to me
and let me
know
love again.

You come to me
making me
whole once more
whispering
words of sweetness
and what would I do
if you
didn't
come to me?

Heart~

Wonderful is life that is
taken with gratitude and
a sincere open heart.

Hope~

Knowledge brings me information
taking me out of the smallness
that is my ego and into the river of hope

Blessings~

I want to swim in your blessings for they up-hold my
highest light.
These feelings that are more than mere feelings elicit
aspirations.
In your light I am new. In your honor I am fresh. I am
young. I am *still...*

I want for you to feel the blessings I send to you in my
heart so reverent.

I want for these blessings to become a part of you as they
are of me.
In this way, I pray that we are merged in our truest form of
love
for your heart is mine and mine is yours.
In our blessings we are 'one.'

It is here that I am clear of who "I" am.
It is here that I am able to transcend
the duality which prevents me from loving fully.
It is here in these blessings that are essentially yours
that I am my "Self." I am alive. I am free!

I pray that you will hold my blessings of love for you.
I pray that these blessings transcend illnesses of the mind
and the body from this world's play.
I pray that these blessings are an asset to healing.
I pray that my blessings become part of your great Mission.
I pray that the blessings of concern which I carry with me
in my very breath, meditation, dreams and soul
are illuminated as you continue to light up my path
with your goodness, grace and bountiful generosity.

You are my truest blessing.
You are the light that I seek.
You are the love that I hold.
You are my prayers.
You are my longing.
You are my life.

In your blessings I am my best.
I am "One" in your blessings.
I am "Om."

You are God's blessing for the world.

The Backyard~

Every once in a while
I remember those days
when we played
in the backyard
dancing to our own songs~
you with your plastic sword
and me with my mud pies.

We laughed
the smiles
of the very young
that once came so easily
and we cried
hidden tears
that concealed
shame
though we'd never tell.

We kept it together
you and I
in between those trees
that shaded us
from grown up
realities.

I slipped in and out
of your toy cars
building cities

with your blocks
and ammunition
with rocks that were ours
as you held onto my hand.

You were my best friend,
my confidant,
my greatest hope~
my brother.

Somehow within the forts
that we built
with rusted nails
we saw the future
and we hid
for just a while
among those trees
in that backyard.

And all these years later
it seems as if suddenly,
like the ships
that old men
cast aside
we abandoned
our toys
moving,
moving
and still moving
into adult days.

I miss that backyard
and I miss you,

~~my brother

Be My Guide~

On the wings of an angel
I held on as tentative
and whispery as his breath
while he flew
with the mighty speed
of one directed by God.

He soared through the majestic
clouds of purples
and sang to me of love.

I knew that his heart was mine
and that I would be guided.
My destiny was made clear
by the love that I had waited for
because when he smiled
and when he cried
 my heart softcncd
and the purpose of my life
was clarified.

I am forever humbled…

Time's Travel~

The dance of the sky's blue
cradled my soul
as streams of consciousness

outlined your face
traveling in time's dreams.

I barely held the glance
penetrating my eyes.

Yet, an impression formed
without explanation or demand,
but a knowingness of trust
that went beyond the travel
through all space and time.

As you recognized
what I tried not to show
and exposed me to my core.
You revealed my vulnerabilities
and loosened
ties that I never knew
existed.

You forced abandonment
of unknown lifetimes through
time's travel.

You danced in merit's fire
while I reveled in yet another
tribulation.
I cried because I didn't understand
why--you bothered--with me.

Honor permeated through the brittle shield
of fear that I clung to
as I screamed to be released.

Yet, like the ocean's fierceness
you held me in time's travel.

And still~
Like a mother you nurture me
Like a friend you console me
Like a lover you take me
                    by the heart
in time's travel.

Still...
I seek that glance
of time that I traveled through
to see your eyes
that vested my soul.

Daughter Of The Moon~

I am
a daughter of the moon
who rules the tides
with thundering, crashing waves
penetrating emotions
thrashing inner turmoils
of heart and mind.

With her fierceness
all is illuminated
leaving nothing hidden;
not even what has been
tucked away in the crevice
of a slightly built vulnerability

can escape the madness
that is this full moon.

With brilliant luminosity
she
embraces wishes
cast in moonlit beams
from imagination, prayers and
heart felt pleas
that she hears
as vows
made
above the stars.

Am I this fortunate?

I walk the trail under her watchful eyes
holding hands
on this path that I love
and seek the wisdom, guidance
and grace of the night
glimmers painted in silver.

I am made aware
that I couldn't fathom
a life without this walk
under her radiant spell
that burns me at times
to a sizzle,
yet, cools
with incandescent rays
beyond my mind

transmitted on her
full moon nights.

I am
a daughter of the moon.

About The Author

Marian Griffin was born in Manhattan, New York and now resides in the San Francisco Bay Area where she is a meditator and a teacher. Marian has been a writer all of her life. Her undergraduate degree is in Advertising/Journalism. She has been graced with an amazing spiritual teacher for going on twenty years who has changed her life's focus and has taught her greater possibilities. Notes From The Heart is Marian's first book.

Soon To Be Published:

"Whatever Happened To Lucy?" is Marian's second book and is a fun fictional account of how one young woman's determination changed the lives of all of those around her.

From a tough background of discard and abuse Lucy was determined to find a way out and Nick Cascades appeared as an "opportunity." However, she wanted more and when she fell in love with the handsome and married politician, Douglas Wilder life was altered forever for her and for his family. This almost destroyed her until Miranda came into her life and changed everything with her heart.

Miranda Wilder was the girl who never gave up on herself, her family and even on complete strangers who she could have easily despised. Miranda did what she felt was the "right" thing to do and with that she changed everyone's lives for the better.

22390675R00142

Made in the USA
Lexington, KY
27 April 2013